# 1888 Sermons

*Presented at the General Conference Session
and the General Conference Institute
which preceded the Session in
Minneapolis, Minnesota*

By
Ellen G. White

**TEACH Services, Inc.**
New York

**PRINTED IN
THE UNITED STATES OF AMERICA**

World rights reserved. This book or any portion thereof may not be copied or reproduced in any form or manner whatever, except as provided by law, without the written permission of the publisher, except by a reviewer who may quote brief passages in a review.

The author assumes full responsibility
for the accuracy of all facts and quotations
as cited in this book.

2005  06  07  08  09  10  11  12  ·  5  4  3  2  1

Copyright © 2000, 2005 TEACH Services, Inc.
ISBN-13: 978-1-57258-130-2
ISBN-10: 1-57258-130-1
Library of Congress Control Number: 98-84190

*Published by*

**TEACH Services, Inc.**
*www.TEACHServices.com*

# Table of Contents

**A Living Connection With God** .............. 1
*Morning Talk, Oct. 11, 1888, MS 6, 1888*

**Tell of God's Love and Power** ............... 5
*Sermon, Oct. 13, 1888, MS 7, 1888*

**The Need of Advancement** ................ 21
*Morning Talk, Oct. 18, 1888*

**Advancing in Christian Experience** ......... 27
*Sabbath, Oct. 20, 1888, MS 8, 1888*

**A Chosen People** ........................ 41
*Sermon, Oct. 21, 1888, MS 17, 1888*

**Counsels to Ministers.** ................... 45
*Discourse to Ministers, Oct. 21, 1888, MS 8a, 1888*

**Remarks on Missionary Work.** .............. 65
*Oct. 23, 1888, MS 10, 1888*

**Morning Talk** ........................... 73
*Oct. 24, 1888, MS 9, 1888*

**Call to a Deeper Study of the Word.** ......... 79
*Nov., 1888, MS 15, 1888*

# A Living Connection With God

*Morning Talk, Oct. 11, 1888, MS 6, 1888*

I am thankful, brethren and sisters, that God has spared me to come to this meeting. I have been sick nigh unto death; but prayer was offered by those assembled at the Oakland camp meeting, and the Lord heard them. It was not by my faith, for I had none, but they exercised faith in my behalf, and the Lord gave me strength to bear my testimony to the people in Oakland, and then I started, as it were, at a venture to come on this journey. I had but one sinking spell on the way, but the Lord helped me, and when we reached Kansas City I went out to the campground where they were holding their meeting and spoke to the people. In this I realize and know that the Lord has strengthened me, and He shall have all the glory.

Now as we have assembled here we want to make the most of our time. I have thought again and again that if we would only make the most of the precious opportunities God had given us, they would do us so much more good; but we too often let them slip away, and we do not realize that benefit from them which we should.

My mind has been directed to the words of the apostle Paul. He says, in the twentieth of Acts, beginning with verse 17: "And from Miletus he sent to Ephesus, and called the elders of the church. And when they were come to him, he said unto them, Ye know, from the first day that I came into Asia, after what manner I have been with you at all seasons, serving the Lord with all humility of mind, and with many tears, and temptations, which befell me by the lying in wait of the Jews: and how I kept back nothing that was profitable unto you, but have shewed you, and have taught you publicly, and from house to house, testifying both to the Jews, and also to the Greeks, repentance toward God, and faith toward our Lord Jesus Christ."

I have thought again and again, brethren and sisters, if we were Bible believers as well as Bible readers, and would carry out just what God has given us, we would be far better than we are at the present time. But we do not realize that it is the loving voice of God speaking to us from His Word. We are to think everything of it and take it home to our hearts. Then Paul goes on to say, in verse 24, "Neither count I my life dear unto myself, so that I might finish my course with joy, and the ministry, which I have received of the Lord Jesus, to testify the gospel of the grace of God." "Wherefore I take you to record this day, that I am pure from the blood of all men. For I have not shunned to declare unto you all the counsel of God" (verses 26, 27). What a testimony is that—"free from the blood of all men."

Now here is the exhortation: "Take heed therefore unto yourselves, and to all the flock, over which the Holy Ghost hath made you overseers, to feed the church of God, which he hath purchased with his own blood." Now what is the necessity of watching them? Why says he, "For I know this, that after my departing shall grievous wolves enter in among you, not sparing the flock" (verses 28, 29).

Brethren, if we would be [in earnest] the power of the Holy Ghost would attend our efforts, and we would see a different state of things among us. We are placed in trust with the most solemn truths ever committed to mortals, but the course of some is of such a character that God cannot answer their prayers. Their prayers are offensive to His holiness, and should He hear and answer their prayers they would be confirmed in a wrong course, and others would be led away from the straight paths. Why cannot we take the truth God has revealed and weave it into our very life and character? If we have the spirit of Christ in our hearts we will have a burden for the perishing souls around us as Paul had, and we will leave such an impression upon the young men and women who claim to believe the truth that they will feel that there are important responsibilities resting upon them. They will feel that their faith must be increased and that they must take up the work lying directly in their pathway, and be a blessing to others—humble, diligent, obedient; and when they meet their associates it will be to talk of Jesus. They will carry Jesus into their homes and testify to all of His mercy.

If Christ is formed within the hope of glory, you will put away all vanity and foolish speaking. You will be sanctified through the truth. You will so labor for God that you can have an approving conscience in your ministerial work, and you can say with the devoted Saint Paul that you are clean from the blood of all men. But you cannot say this unless you are constantly gaining wisdom and knowledge from God as the branch draws nourishment from the living vine, unless His Holy Spirit is resting upon you and you are taking Jesus into your heart, thinking and talking of Jesus, and doing His work wherever you are. This is the only way that we can work successfully in these last times. Christ was Himself the example we should follow, not merely in outward form, but as He was in purity, self-denial, meekness, and love. So we should follow Him in the world. His humiliation, His reproach, His crucifixion, and His cross He gave to His disciples. He also gave to them the glory that was given Him. He said, "He that believeth on me, the works that I do shall he do also; and greater works than these shall he do; because I go unto my Father."

Let us commence right here in this meeting and not wait till the meeting is half through. We want the Spirit of God here now; we need it, and we want it to be revealed in our characters. We want the power of God here, and we want it to shine in our hearts. Brethren, let us take hold of the work as never before. Let us inquire, How is it with my soul? Is it in that condition that it will be well with me? Shall Christ come and find me as I now am? May God help us to be clean in spirit, pure and holy in all manner of conversation and godliness.

## Tell of God's Love and Power

*Sermon, Oct. 13, 1888, MS 7, 1888*

(First page of sermon missing)

How can we understand God? How are we to know our Father? We are to call Him by the endearing name of Father. And how are we to know Him and the power of His love? It is through diligent search of the Scriptures. We cannot appreciate God unless we take into our souls the great plan of redemption. We want to know all about these grand problems of the soul, of the redemption of the fallen race. It is a wonderful thing that after man had violated the law of God and separated himself from God, was divorced, as it were, from God—that after all this there was a plan made whereby man should not perish, but that he should have everlasting life.

After the transgression of Adam in Eden it was Christ whom God gave to us, not that we might be saved in our sins, but that we might be saved from our sins, that we should return to our loyalty to God and become obedient children. As we yield our minds, our souls, our bodies, and our all to the controlling Spirit of God, it is then that the Spirit of truth is with us and we can become intelligent in regard to this great plan of redemption.

It is true that God gave His only-begotten Son to die for us, to suffer the penalty of the [broken] law of God. We are to consider this and dwell upon it. And when our minds are constantly dwelling upon the matchless love of God to the fallen race, we begin to know God, to become acquainted with Him, to have a knowledge of God, and of how Jesus Christ, when He came to our world, laid aside His royal robes and His kingly crown and clothed His divinity with humanity. For our sakes He became poor that we through His poverty might be made rich. The Father sent His Son here, and right here on this little atom of a world were enacted the grandest scenes that were ever known to humanity.

All the universe of heaven was looking on with intense interest. Why? The great battle was to be fought between the power of darkness and the Prince of light. Satan's work was to magnify his power constantly. Where was his power? He claimed to be the prince of the world and he exercised his power over the inhabitants of the world. Satan's power was exercised in such a masterly manner that they would not acknowledge God. Satan wanted that the children of men should get such an idea of his wonderful work that they would talk of his masterly power. In doing this he was all the time placing God in a false light. He was presenting Him as a God of injustice, and not a God of mercy. He was constantly stirring up their minds so that they would have an incorrect view of God.

How was God to be rightly represented to the world? How was it to be known that He was a God of love, full of mercy, kindness, and pity? How was the world to know this? God sent His Son, and He was to represent to the world the character of God.

Satan has come right in and placed himself between God and man. It is his work to divert the human mind, and he throws his dark shadow right athwart our pathways, so that we cannot discern between God and the moral darkness and corruption and the mass of iniquity that is in our world. Then what are we going to do about the matter? Shall we let that darkness remain?—No. There is a power here for us that will bring in the light of heaven to our dark world. Christ has been in heaven and He will bring the light of heaven, drive back the darkness, and let the sunlight of His glory in. Then we shall see, amid the corruption and pollution and defilement, the light of heaven.

## Tell of God's Love and Power

We must not give up at the defilement that is in the human race and ever keep that before the mind's eye. We must not look at that. What then are we to do? What is our work?—To behold "what manner of love the Father hath bestowed upon us." Do not let the blighting influences that are flooding the world be the picture that is before the mind, but hold up the purity and love of God. Do not hang in memory's hall pictures of all the corruption and iniquity that you can bundle together. No, do not do it. It discourages the mind. A discouraged man is good for nothing. Just get the mind off these dark pictures by talking of God's love, and you may hang memory's halls with the brightest pictures that you can imagine.

We want to keep the perfect Pattern before us. God was so good as to send a representation of Himself in His Son Jesus Christ, and we want to get the mind and heart to unfold and reach upward. Just as soon as Adam and Eve fell, their countenances fell at the sight of their miserableness. We may see our wretchedness, and we should pray that God will reveal our own hearts to us; but we should pray also that He will reveal Himself to us as a sin-pardoning Redeemer. Let yours be the prayer, Reveal Thyself to me, that in Thy matchless grace I may lay hold on the golden link, Christ, which has been let down from heaven to earth, that I may grasp it and be drawn upward.

Brethren, you have all seen on the bosom of the lake the beautiful white lily. How anxious we have been, how we have wished and worked, that we might get that blossom. No matter how much scum and debris and filth there is around it, yet that does not destroy our desire for the lily. We wonder how the lily can be so beautiful and white where there is so much filth. Well, there is a stem that strikes down to the golden sands beneath and gathers nothing but the purest substance that feeds the lily until it develops into the pure and spotless flower as we see it.

Should not this teach us a lesson? It ought to. It shows that although there is iniquity all around us we should not approach it. Do not talk of the iniquity and wickedness that are in the world, but elevate your minds and talk of your Saviour. When you see iniquity all around you it makes you all the more glad that He is your Saviour, and we are His children. Then, shall we look at the iniquity around us and dwell upon the dark side? You cannot cure it; then talk of something that is higher, better, and more noble. Talk of those things that will leave a good impression on the mind, and will lift every soul up out of this iniquity into the light beyond.

Now, we may go into a cellar and stay there and look around into its dark corners, and we can talk of the darkness and say, "Oh, it is so dark here," and keep talking about it. But will it make it any lighter? Oh no! What are you going to do? Come out of it; come out of the dark into the upper chamber where the light of God's countenance shines brightly.

You know our bodies are made up of the food assimilated. Now, it is the same with our minds. If we have a mind to dwell on the disagreeable things of life, it will not give us any hope, but we want to dwell on the cheery scenes of heaven. Says Paul, "Our light affliction, which is but for a moment, worketh for us a far more exceeding and eternal weight of glory."

While we were in Switzerland I had many letters from a sister whom I dearly love and highly esteem. In every one of these letters were the most gloomy pictures. She seemed to be dwelling on everything objectionable. Soon after I received these letters I prayed the Lord that He would give her help to turn her mind from the channel that it was running in. That night I had a dream presented to me three times. I was walking in a beautiful garden, and Sister Martha_____was by my side. As soon as she came into the garden I said, "Martha, do you not see this beautiful garden? See, here are the lilies, the roses, and the pinks." "Yes," she said, as she looked up and smiled. Soon I looked to see where she was. I was looking at the lilies, the roses, and the pinks, and did not see her. She was in another part of the garden, and was grasping a thistle. Then she was pricking her hands on the bramblebushes. She said they hurt her hands, and she asked, "Why do they keep all these thistles and these briers in the garden? Why do they let them stay here?"

Then there appeared before us a tall, dignified man who said, "Gather the roses, the lilies, and the pinks; discard the brambles and touch them not." Then I awoke, and when I went to sleep I dreamed the very same thing again. Three times I had the same dream, and I arose—because I could not sleep—and wrote to Sister Martha the dream I had had.

Now, said I, God does not want you to gather up everything objectionable; He wants you to look at His wonderful works and at His purity. He wants you to take a view of His matchless love and His power, to look up through the beauties of nature to nature's God. Said I, This [dream] represents your case exactly. You are dwelling on the dark side. You are talking of those things that give no light and bring no joy into your life. But you must turn your mind from these things to God. There are enough roses, pinks, and lilies in the garden of God's love so that you need not look at the briers, the thistles, and the brambles. Now, I did not see these things because I was delighting myself with the flowers and all the beauties of the garden.

Now, that is what we want to do, brethren. We want to have our minds on the encouraging things. We want to have our minds on the new country to which we are to be introduced. Our citizenship is not of this world, but it is above, and we want to consider what characters we should possess in order to become inhabitants of that better world and associates of the saints of God in heaven.

Sister Martha took it, and her soul was lifted above discouragement. Now, I do not want Satan to succeed in throwing his dark shadow across your pathway. I want you to get away from that shadow. The Man of Calvary will throw the light of His love across your pathway and dispel the darkness. He is able to do it and will do it, for He is Lord of all. Somebody has thrown His light around you; it is Jesus Christ.

I remember when my sister Sarah, now sleeping in the grave, who attended me in my first travels, was in discouragement. She said, "I had a strange dream last night. I dreamed somebody opened the door and I was afraid of him; and as I continued to look at him he increased in size and filled the whole space from the floor to the ceiling, and I continued to grow more and more afraid. Then I thought that I had Jesus, and I said, 'I have Jesus; I am not afraid of you.' Then he began to shrink and shrink until you could scarcely see him, and he went out of the door."

It taught her a lesson. She said, "Ellen, we talk a great deal more of the power of the devil than we have any right to. It pleases him, and his satanic majesty is honored; he exults over it, and we give him honor in doing this; but," she said, "I am going to talk of Jesus, of His love, and tell of His power." And so she brought her soul right out of darkness and discouragement into light, and she bore a living testimony for God and heaven.

Now, I think our testimony would be a great deal better if we talked more of Jesus and His love and did not pay so much honor to the devil. Why should we not do it? Why not let the light of Jesus shine in our hearts?

I remember that when I was in Oakland there was a sister who was in great trouble. She said, "My mother troubles me. My father is a good man; but my mother has her eyes fixed on so many young couples where the husband is disloyal that she seems to think her husband and everyone else is disloyal. I do not know what she will do or drive him to. She thinks he is unfaithful, and she talks of it and dwells upon it till she brings all her misery on the rest of us, as though she were imposed upon, when there is no need of it at all."

## Tell of God's Love and Power

Is not this the case with many of us? Do we not dwell on trifles and talk of them till our thoughts are changed to the same similitude? We can drive even our children to do wrong things by accusing them of wrongs of which they are not guilty. While we are to rebuke and exhort in all love, should we not also exalt Jesus and talk of His love?

"Behold, what manner of love the Father hath bestowed upon us, that we should be called the sons of God." It is one of Satan's devices that we should be picking up all these disagreeable things and that our minds should not be dwelling on God and His love. That is what Satan wants, that we should keep our minds occupied with these things of a revolting character that cannot bring peace, joy, and harmony into the life—nothing but discouragement—and that we should not represent Jesus Christ.

Now, Christ left us His work when He went away, and He said, "Lo, I am with you always, even unto the end of the world." We are not left alone in the hands of the devil. Do you think our heavenly Father would leave us alone to carry on the work of redemption and bringing up the fallen race, that He would leave us in a world flooded with evil with no help, no support, after He had endured the agonies of the cross? Do you think He will leave us now?—No! Says the Saviour, "Lo, I am with you always, even unto the end of the world." And again, "If I go away I will come again." "If ye shall ask any thing in my name, I will do it." This is on the condition that we keep His commandments. Is not this a blessed promise? Why do we not talk of it more and praise God for it? Here are the precious promises of the Word of God to us, and why do we not take them?

Now I want to read to you something about this love of God, and what we ought to do in order that we shall bring joy into our own hearts. Paul says, "For this cause we also, since the day we heard it, do not cease to pray for you, and to desire that ye might be filled with the knowledge of his will in all wisdom and spiritual understanding." Not in order that we might have a taste, but that we might be filled. "That ye might walk worthy of the Lord unto all pleasing, being fruitful in every good work, and increasing in the knowledge of God. Strengthened [with] all might, according to his glorious power, unto all patience and longsuffering with joyfulness."

If we have a sense of the goodness of God in sending His Son to die for sinful man, and if we keep that interwoven into our experience and riveted in the mind, we shall have such love for those for whom Christ died that there will be no [desire for] supremacy. It is Satan that brings in these differences. While we are worshipping God there will be no hatred, no envy, no evil surmising. Brethren, we have no time for these. We cannot think of them. There is something else before us. It is the eternal weight of glory, the plan of salvation. We ought to understand it from beginning to the close, that we may present it justly to the world.

What is our work here? We are to take hold of the work just where Christ left it. What was His work? To reveal the Father to us. What is our work? To reveal Christ to the world. How can we do this? By talking of the devil? Oh no, we have a better work to do. We want to talk of the crucified and risen Saviour. Oh, what a terrible thing it would be for any of us to profess to be followers of Jesus Christ and then make a botch of it, and He find us with characters all stained with defilement. What a fearful responsibility rests upon us! How is Christ to be revealed to the world, unless it is through those who take hold on His merits, who believe in Jesus Christ, to the saving of their souls? He cleanseth me. He cleanseth me from the defilement of sin. And here let the sound be heard of what Christ has done for me. There is liberty for the sons of God. There is a wide place for my feet to stand on, and we may have the fullness of the love of God in our hearts.

I thank God that Christ has died for me and that I have been brought through a terrible ordeal of sickness and suffering of mind. It seemed as though the enemy cast a cloud of darkness between me and

## Tell of God's Love and Power

my Saviour, and for twelve days it seemed that I could think of nothing but my sufferings. When I came to Oakland my heart was so weak and feeble that it seemed that a stone was lying on it. Not a particle of joy was there in it; not an emotion of gladness could I realize. But was I to think that heaven was closed to me? No! I must take the Bible, and I took the Bible and walked right out by faith, and the darkness separated from me.

When I awake in the night I begin to pray. Some three weeks ago I awoke and said, "O God, have mercy on me." I had no more than spoken when a voice by me seemed to say, "I am right by you, I have not left you." This was everything to me, and it may be just the same to you. Jesus says, I am right by you, dwelling with you, you are not alone at all. That was just the joy I experienced, and it was worth more than mountains of gold to me. I have learned to trust my Saviour, and I want to tell you that I have a Saviour, and He lives; and because He lives I shall live also.

Our lives are hid with Christ in God, and when He who is our Life shall appear, we shall appear with Him in glory. You do not need to be discouraged. Christ came to save His people from their sins. The devil will come to you and tell you that you are a sinner and cannot be saved. But Christ says He came to save sinners, and there you can meet the devil every time. Christ can pardon your sins. He says, "Come now, and let us reason together...: though your sins be as scarlet, they shall be as white as snow; though they be red like crimson, they shall be as wool."

Oh, I want you to take the rich promises of God and hang memory's halls with them. What more could you want than that promise? We have the assurance that a mother can forget her nursing child but He will not forget us. Oh, I want the promises of God to be the living pictures on memory's walls, that you can look at them. Then your heart can be filled with His grace and you may exalt Jesus and crown Him Lord of all. That is your privilege.

Now I want to read Colossians 1:12: "Giving thanks unto the Father, which hath made us meet to be partakers of the inheritance of the saints in light." There is something to be patient and long-suffering over—"who hath delivered us from the power of darkness." Yes, we should talk of deliverance, not of bondage; we should be joyful and not cast down. "And hath translated us into the kingdom of his dear Son." Why can we not act as subjects of His kingdom? May the love of Christ burn on the altar of our hearts, and may you love Christ as your Saviour, and your brethren as yourself.

"In whom we have redemption through his blood, even the forgiveness of sin." Now we want to act like individuals who are redeemed by the blood of Christ; we are to rejoice in the blood of Christ and in the forgiveness of sins. That is what we are to do, and may God help us to get our minds off the dark pictures, and think on those things that will give us light.

Now I want to read another scripture: "Be careful for nothing." What does that mean? Why, don't cross a bridge before you get to it. Don't make a time of trouble before it comes. You will get to it soon enough, brethren. We are to think of today, and if we do well the duties of today, we will be ready for the duties of tomorrow. "But in everything by prayer and supplication with thanksgiving let your requests be made known unto God." Thanksgiving is to be brought in. "And the peace of God, which passeth all understanding, shall keep your hearts and minds through Christ Jesus." Then we are not given over into the hands of the devil; we have a loving heavenly Father, and He has given His Son to bear our iniquity.

Now what is next? "Finally, brethren." Now, this is to each of you. It comes along down the line to our times. "Finally, brethren, whatsoever things are true, whatsoever things are honest, whatsoever things are just, whatsoever things are pure, whatsoever things are lovely, whatsoever things are of good report; if there be any virtue, if there be any praise, think on these things." Shall we do it? Shall we turn over a page in our religious experience and train and educate the mind so that it will not take these things that are disagreeable and think on them? Shall we think on these things that give us no power, or shall we let our minds dwell on those things that will give us a better feeling toward our brethren and elevate our souls to God? Now, there are many things that we need to bring into our lives and characters. May God help us that we may take these things to our hearts and think of them, that our minds may be elevated above earthly things.

We have seen of the grace of God since we met you last. Since last spring I have visited Lemoore, Fresno, and Selma. I was at the Selma camp meeting. During my stay there I was introduced to a tall man—over six feet tall—and well proportioned. When he took my hand he seemed much affected and said, "I am so glad to meet you; I am thankful that I can speak with you." After going into the tent a brother came in and said, "That man has a history." Then he went on and told how a year before he had been converted; how he had once kept the Sabbath but had gone back, and how he claimed that he never had been converted. Then after he gave up the truth he went back into the company of hard cases, and Satan took complete possession of him. Two or three were linked with him in his wickedness—men who would not want it to be known that they were in such business. They stole and did wickedness in every way.

He was not a licentious man; he had a wife and he respected her. She was a Sabbathkeeper, and he would not allow a word to be said against her. This was the position he took; he loved her, but not enough to stop his evil course. He did not care for the spoil of his robberies, but did it for the enjoyment he found in it. Well, Elder [E. P.] Daniels was holding meetings, and he was speaking on confession. What was said seemed to take hold of this man's mind, and he could not resist. He seemed to turn white, and then left the tent. He could not stand it. He went out and then he came back again. This he did three times; he looked as if he were going to faint away.

After the meeting had closed he said, "I must talk to you, sir." He told Elder Daniels his condition and said, "Is there any hope for me? I am a lost man; I am undone; I am a sinner. Will you pray for me? I dare not leave this place to go home for fear the Lord will cut me down in my sins." He said he could not stay in the tent, and went out again and again, but did not dare remain outside for fear the power of the devil should fasten on him and that would be the last of him.

They prayed for him, and the man was converted right there. The defiant look was gone; his countenance was changed. "Now," said he, "I have a work to do. I stole thirty-one sheep from that man in Selma, and I must go and confess to him." Elder Daniels was afraid to have it known for fear they would shut him up. He said he would rather go to prison and stay there than to think that Christ had not forgiven his sin. So he started, with a young man who before this was engaged with him in thefts, to go and see the man. He met the man on the road and stopped him. The man commenced to shake like an aspen leaf. He was an infidel. Well, he got on his knees before them in the road and begged to be forgiven. The man asked, "Where did you get this? What has brought you into this state? I did not know that there was any such religion as this." They told him that they had been down to the camp meeting, and heard it preached there. "Well," said he, "I will go over to that meeting."

They confessed to having burned houses and barns. And they went to the grand jury and confessed to having stolen here and there. Mind, they confessed to the authorities. They said, "We deliver ourselves up. Do with us as you see fit." So the case was considered in court, and they had a council over the matter. One suggested that they better put those men through. The judge looked at him and said, "What, put him through? Put a man through that God is putting through? Would

## Tell of God's Love and Power

you take hold of a man that God is taking hold of? Whom God's forgiving power has taken hold of? Would you do that? No, I would rather have my right arm cut off to the shoulder." Something got hold of those men so that they all wept as children.

The report of that experience went everywhere. People thought that there was a power in this truth that was in nothing else—a power that shows that Jesus lives. We have seen the power of His grace manifested in many cases in a remarkable manner.

Now, whenever we can see anything encouraging, put it in the paper, and talk about it. Why talk of Satan's great power and his wonderful works, and say nothing of the majesty and goodness and mercy of our God which falls to the ground unnoticed? Pick these up, brethren, with consecrated hands, pick them up. Hold them high before the world. Talk of the love of God and dwell upon it; thank Him for it. Open the doors of your hearts and show forth your gratitude and love. Clear away this rubbish which Satan has piled before the door of your heart and let Jesus come in and occupy. Talk of His goodness and power.

You know how it was with Moses. He felt that he must have an answer to his prayer. He realized the responsibility of leading the people out of Egypt, but he did not go and pick up everything objectionable and dwell on it. He knew they were a stiff-necked people, and he said, "Lord, I must have Thy presence"; and the Lord said, "My presence shall go with thee." You remember Moses went into the wilderness and stayed forty years, during which time he put away self, and that made room so that he could have the presence of God with him.

He thought if he could have the presence of God's glory it would help him to carry on this great work. He says, "Shew me thy glory." Now that was a man of faith, and God did not rebuke him. God did not call it presumption, but He took that man of faith and put him into the cleft of the rock and put His hand over the rock and showed him all the glory that he could endure. He made His goodness to pass before him, and showed him His goodness, His mercy, and His love. If we want God's glory to pass before us, if we want to have memory's halls hung with the promises of love and mercy, we want to talk of His glory and tell of His power. And if we have dark and miserable days we can commit these promises to memory and take our minds off discouragement. It would please the devil to think he has bothered us; but we want to talk of Jesus and His love and His power, because we have nothing better to talk of.

Now, brethren and sisters, let us hope in God. Let gratitude enter into our hearts, and while we may have to bear plain testimony to separate from sin and iniquity, we do not want to be hammering upon that string forever. We want to lift up these souls that are cast down; we want them to catch that love of God and know that He will put His everlasting arms beneath them. Brethren and sisters, we want to look up; not down, but upward, upward, lifting the soul higher and still higher. I want these blessings and I will not rest satisfied until I am filled with all the fullness of God. Nothing can be greater than that, can it? We want to be in that position where we shall perfect a Christian character and represent Jesus Christ to the world. Christ was sent as our pattern and shall we not show that we have all His love and kindness and all His charms? And the love of Jesus Christ will take possession of our characters and our lives, and our conversation will be holy, and we will dwell on heavenly things.

I believe that Jesus is interested in all this assembly. He is here today. He says, "Where two or three are gathered together in my name, there am I in the midst of them." He is with you and that to bless. We want the blessing, and why should we not have it? We are to meet the moral darkness that is in the world, and we must meet it as Christ did. We must reveal Christ to all who are around us. When we do this work we are abiding in Christ and Christ is abiding in us, not only

## Tell of God's Love and Power

when we speak of Him, but He is with us all the time to help us on every point, to press back the power of moral darkness.

"Fear not, little flock; for it is your Father's good pleasure to give you the kingdom." He is not your enemy, He is your best Friend, and He wishes us to show to the world that we have a God. He wants us to show that we have Jesus with us, and He is stronger than the strong man armed. Therefore, let us elevate our minds and our conversation and seek for heaven and heavenly things. God help us when we are in this position, that we shall not be seeking after earthly things, but that we shall be charmed with the things of heaven. We want to "behold, what manner of love the Father hath bestowed upon us, that we should be called the sons of God: therefore the world knoweth us not, because it knew him not. Beloved, now are we the sons of God, and it doth not yet appear what we shall be: but we know that, when he shall appear, we shall be like him; for we shall see him as he is."

I look over this congregation, and you look like discouraged men, like men who have been fighting with the powers of darkness; but courage, brethren! There is hope! "It doth not yet appear what we shall be: but we know that, when he shall appear, we shall be like him; for we shall see him as he is. And every man that hath this hope in him purifieth himself, even as he is pure."

Oh, I love Him. I love Him, for He is my love. I see in Him matchless charms, and oh, how I want that we shall enter in through the gates into the city. Then shall every crown be taken off from every head and cast at the feet of Jesus our blessed Redeemer. He has purchased it for me; He has purchased it for you, and we shall acknowledge Him Lord of all. And we shall cast all our honor at His feet and crown Him Lord of all. We shall shout, "Glory to God in the highest." I wish we would learn to praise Him more. "Whoso offereth praise glorifieth God." I wish you would talk of it. I wish you would educate your hearts and lips to praise Him, to talk of His power and glory. I wish you would tell of His power. When you do it you are elevating your Saviour, and when you lift that standard up against your enemy he will flee from you. God help us to praise Him more and to be found faultless.

## The Need of Advancement

*Morning Talk, Oct. 18, 1888,
RH, October 8, 1889*

I hope that at the beginning of this meeting our hearts may be impressed with the positive statement of our Saviour, "Without me ye can do nothing." We have a great and solemn truth committed to us for these last days, but a mere assent to and belief in this truth will not save us. The principles of the truth must be interwoven with our character and life. We should cherish every ray of light that falls upon our pathway, and live up to the requirements of God. We should grow in spirituality. We are losing a great deal of the blessing we might have at this meeting, because we do not take advance steps in the Christian life, as our duty is presented before us; and this will be an eternal loss.

If we had a just appreciation of the importance and greatness of our work, and could see ourselves as we are at this time, we should be filled with wonder that God could use us, unworthy as we are, in the work of bringing souls into the truth. There are many things that we ought to be able to understand, that we do not comprehend because we are so far behind our privileges. Christ said to his disciples, "I have yet many things to say unto you, but ye cannot bear them now." This is our condition. Would they not have been able to understand what he had to say to them, if they had been doers of his word—if they had improved point after point of the truth which he had presented to them? But although they could not then understand, he told them that he would send the Comforter, who would lead them into all truth. We should be in a position where we can comprehend the teaching, leading, and working of the Spirit of Christ. We must not measure God or his truth by our finite understanding, or by our preconceived opinions.

There are many who do not realize where they are standing; for they are spiritually blinded. "Examine yourselves, whether ye be in the faith; prove your own selves. Know ye not your own selves, how that Jesus Christ is in you, except ye be reprobates?" I trust that none of us will be found to be reprobates. Is Christ abiding in your hearts by faith? Is his Spirit in you? If it is, there will be such a yearning in your soul for the salvation of those for whom Christ has died, that self will sink into insignificance, and Christ alone will be exalted. Brethren and sisters, there is great need at this time of humbling ourselves before God, that the Holy Spirit may come upon us.

There are many who are content with a superficial knowledge of the truth. The precious truths for this time are brought out so clearly in our publications, that many are satisfied, and do not search the Scriptures for themselves. They do not meditate upon the statements made, and bring every proposition to the law and to the testimony, to see if their ideas correspond to the word of God. Many do not feel that it is essential for them to compare scripture with scripture, and spiritual things with spiritual; and therefore they do not grow in grace and in the knowledge of the truth, as it is their privilege to do. They accept the truth, without any deep conviction of sin, and present themselves as laborers in the cause of God when they are unconverted men. One says, "I want to do something in the cause of truth;" another says, "I want to enter the ministry;" and as our brethren are very anxious to get all the laborers they can, they accept these men without considering whether their lives give evidence that they have a saving knowledge of Christ. No one should be accepted as a laborer in the sacred cause of God, until he makes manifest that he has a real, living experience in the things of God. One reason why the church is in a backslidden state is, that so

## The Need of Advancement

many have come into the truth in this way, and have never known what it is to have the converting power of God upon their souls.

There are many ministers who have never been converted. They come to the prayer-meeting and pray the same old, lifeless prayers over and over; they preach the same dry discourses over and over, from week to week, and from month to month. They have nothing new and inspiring to present to their congregations, and it is evident that they are not eating the flesh and drinking the blood of the Son of man, for they have no life in them. They are not partakers of the divine nature; Christ is not abiding in their hearts by faith.

Those who profess to be united to Christ, should be laborers together with God. The people of God are to warn the world, and to prepare a people to stand in the day of wrath when the Son of man shall come in the clouds of heaven. The members of the church of Christ should gather up the divine rays of light from Jesus, and reflect them to others, leaving a bright track heavenward in the world. They are to be as the wise virgins, having their lamps trimmed and burning, representing the character of Christ to the world. We are not to be satisfied with anything short of this. We are not to be satisfied with our own righteousness, and content without the deep movings of the Spirit of God.

Christ says, "Without me ye can do nothing." It is this marked nothingness, so apparent in the labors of many who profess to be preaching the truth, that alarms us; for we know that this is an evidence that they have not felt the converting power of Christ upon their hearts. You may look from the topmost bough to the lowest branch of their work, and you will find nothing but leaves. God desires us to come up to a higher standard. It is not his will that we should have such a dearth of spirituality. There are some young men that say they have given themselves to the work, who need a genuine experience in the things of God before they are fit to labor in the cause of Christ. Instead of going without the camp, bearing reproach for Christ's sake; instead of seeking the hard places, and trying to bring souls into the truth, these beginners settle themselves in an easy position to visit those who are far advanced in experience. They labor with those who are more capable of teaching them than they are of teaching others. They go from church to church, picking out the easy places, eating and drinking, and suffering others to wait upon them. When you look to see what they have done, there is nothing but leaves. They bring in the report, "I preached here, and I preached there;" but where are the sheaves they have garnered? Where are the souls that have embraced the truth through their efforts? Where is the evidence of their piety and devotion? Those who are bringing the churches up to a higher standard, by earnest efforts as soldiers of Jesus Christ, are doing a good work.

Too often the churches have been robbed by the class I have mentioned; for they take their support from the treasury, and bring nothing in return. They are continually drawing out the means that should be devoted to the support of worthy laborers. There should be a thorough investigation of the cases of those who present themselves to labor in the cause. The apostle warns you to "lay hands suddenly on no man." If the life is not what God can accept, the labors will be worthless; but if Christ is abiding in the heart by faith, every wrong will be made right, and those who are soldiers of Christ will be willing to prove it by a well ordered life. There many who enter the ministry, and their influence demoralizes the churches; and when they are rejected, they take their dismissal as a personal wrong. They have not Christ in the soul, as a well of water springing up unto everlasting life.

I want to exhort those who are in positions of responsibility, to waken to their duty, and not imperil the cause of present truth by engaging inefficient men to do the work of God. We want men who are willing to go into new fields, and to do hard service for the Lord. I remember visiting in Iowa when the country was new, and I saw the farmers breaking the new ground. I noticed that they had heavy teams, and made tremendous efforts to make deep furrows, but the laborers gained strength and muscle by the exercise of their physical powers. It will make our young men strong to go into new fields, and break up the fallow ground of men's hearts. This work will drive them nearer to God. It will help them to see that they are altogether inefficient in themselves. They must be wholly the Lord's. They must put away their self-esteem and self-importance, and put on the Lord Jesus Christ. When they do this, they will be willing to go without the camp, and bear the burden as good soldiers of the cross. They will gain efficiency and ability by mastering difficulties and overcoming obstacles. Men are wanted for responsible positions, but they must be men who have given full proof of their ministry in willingness to wear the yoke of Christ. Heaven regards this class with approval.

I exhort you to have the eye-salve, that you may discern what God would have you do. There are too many Christless sermons preached. An array of powerless words only confirms the people in their backslidings. May God help us that His Spirit may be made manifest among us. We should not wait until we go home to obtain the blessing of Heaven. The Ministers should begin right here with the people to seek God, and to work from the right stand-point. Those who have been long in the work, have been far too content to wait for the showers of the latter rain to revive them. We are the people who, like John, are to prepare the way of the Lord; and if we are prepared for the second coming of Christ, we must work with all diligence to prepare others for Christ's second advent, as did the forerunner of Christ for His first advent, calling men to repentance. The truth of God must be brought into the soul temple, to cleanse and purify it from all defilement. May God help us to search the Scriptures for ourselves, and when we are all filled with the truth of God, it will flow out as water from a living spring. We cannot exhaust the heavenly fountain, and the more we draw, the more we shall delight to draw from the living waters. O may we be converted! We want the Ministers and the young men to be converted. We want to lift up the standard. Let all the people come up to the high calling of God in Christ Jesus. Let us pray that we may hunger and thirst after righteousness; for Jesus says, "Blessed are they which do hunger and thirst after righteousness: for they shall be filled."

# Advancing in Christian Experience

*Sabbath, October 20, 1888, MS 8, 1888*

"Simon Peter, a servant and an apostle of Jesus Christ, to them that have obtained like precious faith with us through the righteousness of God and our Saviour Jesus Christ: Grace and peace be multiplied unto you through the knowledge of God, and of Jesus our Lord, according as his divine power hath given unto us all things that pertain unto life and godliness, through the knowledge of him that hath called us to glory and virtue: whereby are given unto us exceeding great and precious promises: that by these ye might be partakers of the divine nature, having escaped the corruption that is in the world through lust. And beside this, giving all diligence, add to your faith virtue; and to virtue knowledge; and to knowledge temperance; and to temperance patience; and to patience godliness; and to godliness brotherly kindness; and to brotherly kindness charity. For if these things be in you, and abound, they make you that ye shall neither be barren nor unfruitful in the knowledge of our Lord Jesus Christ. But he that lacketh these things is blind, and cannot see afar off, and hath forgotten that he was purged from his old sins. Wherefore the rather, brethren, give diligence to make your calling and election sure: for if ye do these things, ye shall never fall: for so an entrance shall be ministered unto you abundantly into the everlasting kingdom of our Lord and Saviour Jesus Christ. Wherefore I will not be negligent to put you always in remembrance of these things, though ye know them, and be established in the present truth." 2 Peter 1:1–12.

Now mark, it is these graces, this righteousness, that is to be constantly added; and if these things be in you and abound, they make you that you shall be neither barren nor unfruitful in the knowledge of the Lord Jesus Christ.

Now here is subject matter that we might dwell upon, and subject matter for many discourses; but we want to present merely a few ideas to your mind at this time, and we want you to see the necessity of progress. You cannot be a fruitful Christian and have a knowledge of our Lord and Saviour Jesus Christ unless you are a practical Christian, unless you are making progress all the time in divine life. This is all important. Many seem to think that as soon as they go down into the water and receive baptism, and their names are entered upon the church book, then the work is all done. They might have tasted of the knowledge of the world to come; they might have received the evidence that they are children of God; but they cannot retain it unless they go on making progress.

It is impossible for them to obtain a knowledge of Jesus Christ and of His light and knowledge, unless they are advancing and are learners, adding grace to grace. If they do not bring into their households practical religion they will soon lose it all; and they will go into the meeting and carry through a form, and pray and exhort, and perhaps hold some office in the church; but unless they are making advancement all the time there is a decided want, and they will swing back to their old position of ungodliness, just like any other sinner. It is important that we keep all the time adding grace to grace, and if we will work upon the plan of addition, God will work on the plan of multiplication; and just as fast as we add God multiplies His graces unto us.

Those who live doing the works of the enemy, yet bearing the name of the Lord, are lying; they profess to believe the Bible, yet they are working right away from it in their lives and character. In the place of representing Jesus in the character that they shall give to the

## Advancing in Christian Experience

world, they represent the works of Satan, the works of darkness. Now any such names that may be on your church books, although they may give of their means to help to sustain the church, notwithstanding all that, they are stumbling blocks to the church every day they are in it.

Now, what we want to present is how you may advance in the divine life. We hear many excuses: I cannot live up to this or that. What do you mean by this or that? Do you mean that it was an imperfect sacrifice that was made for the fallen race upon Calvary, that there is not sufficient grace and power granted us that we may work away from our own natural defects and tendencies, that it was not a whole Saviour that was given us? [Or] do you mean to cast reproach upon God? Well, you say, it was Adam's sin. You say, I am not guilty of that, and I am not responsible for his guilt and fall. Here all these natural tendencies are in me, and I am not to blame if I act out these natural tendencies. Who is to blame? Is God? Why did God let Satan have this power over human nature? These are accusations against the God of heaven, and He will give you an opportunity, if you want it, of finally bringing your accusations against Him. Then He will bring His accusations against you when you are brought into His court of judgment.

How is it that He is pleading, "I know all the evils and temptations with which you are beset, and I sent My Son Jesus Christ to your world to reveal to you My power, My mightiness; to reveal to you that I am God, and that I will give you help in order to lift you from the power of the enemy, and give you a chance that you might win back the moral image of God." God sent His Son, who was as Himself, one with the Father, and He bore insult and shame and mockery for us, and suffered at last the ignominious death upon Calvary. Satan met Him with opposition just as soon as He came into the world; but He met it all; He did not swerve a bit. Had it not been for the power that God gave Him, He could not have stood the assaults of the enemy; but He did, and although He had him to meet at every step, and was pressed step by step, yet here was the battle fought in this world with the powers of darkness.

Why was not the devil destroyed? Why do you ask such a question? Did not God know what was best? Would it not have destroyed confidence in God? Would it not have cast a reflection upon God if He had destroyed him, him that had taken hold of the very heart of the universe, and the world that was created? The only way to show the disposition of Satan was to give him a chance to develop himself as one who would be worthy of condemnation and death. So the God of heaven, while He did not destroy Satan, gave His Son to counteract the influence of Satan; and when He gave His Son He gave Himself, and here was the image of God that was brought to our world. What for? That we might become mighty with God.

Christ had to meet the enemy. What had he [Satan] been doing prior to Christ's coming to this earth? Why, he had been trying to gain the hearts of evil men and evil women. When Christ came to our world Satan had been working with all the deceptive powers that he could command with his angels to gain the hearts of evil men and women, and combined with Satan they will work on the children of disobedience; and it seems that when Christ made His appearance in our world that Satan had planted himself on the throne as the sovereign of this world. He had the control of human minds. He had taken the human bodies and wrought upon them so that they were possessed with demons. He wrought upon them so that the moral image of God was almost obliterated in them. He was weaving himself into the Jewish nation, and they were led captive and would not acknowledge Christ as the Son of God, notwithstanding the mighty evidences which accompanied Him.

Now Christ takes the field and commences to press back this power of moral darkness. In Luke He announces what His work is to be. "The Spirit of the Lord is upon me, because he hath anointed me to

## Advancing in Christian Experience

preach the gospel to the poor; he hath sent me to heal the brokenhearted, to preach deliverance to the captives, and recovering of sight to the blind, to set at liberty them that are bruised, to preach the acceptable year of the Lord" (Luke 4:18, 19). Even while Christ announced His mission and "all bare him witness, and wondered at the gracious words which proceeded out of his mouth," Satan was on the ground. And there is no meeting but that he is there, and as the truth is being impressed on minds, Satan presents the difficulties.

Christ said, "This day is this scripture fulfilled in your ears." But a state of unbelief arose and the questions began to come up, Is not this the son of Joseph and Mary? What is this that He claims? Is not this Joseph's son? We have seen Him walking with His father to the carpenter shop. "And he said unto them, Ye will surely say unto me this proverb, Physician, heal thyself: whatsoever we have heard done in Capernaum, do also here in thy country. And he said, Verily I say unto you, No prophet is accepted in his own country. But I tell you of a truth, many widows were in Israel in the days of Elias, when the heaven was shut up three years and six months, when great famine was throughout all the land; but unto none of them was Elias sent, save unto Sarepta, a city of Sidon, unto a woman that was a widow. And many lepers were in Israel in the time of Eliseus the prophet; and none of them was cleansed, saving Naaman the Syrian" (verses 23–27).

Now this widow was a heathen woman. God did not send Elijah to those who were in Samaria. Why? Because they had great light, blessings, and privileges, and did not live up to them. And because they had had this great light and had not lived up to it, they were the most hardhearted people in the world, the hardest to impress with the truth. They were not susceptible to the influences of the Spirit of God. There were many lepers in Israel, and none of them were cleansed save Naaman, the Syrian. What was the matter? He who had lived up to the light that he had was in a more favorable position before God than those on whom He had bestowed great light, power, and spiritual advantages, and yet their lives did not correspond to their advantages and privileges.

What did the people do [with Christ] in their madness? They "rose up, and thrust him out of the city." Could their eyes have been opened they would have beheld angels of God all around Him, that all heaven was engaged in this warfare between Christ and the prince of the powers of this world. They could have seen this, but their eyes were holden that they might not see it.

Here I want to tell you what a terrible thing it is if God gives light, and it is impressed on your heart and spirit, for you to do as they did. God will withdraw His Spirit unless His truth is accepted. But Christ was accepted by some; the witness was there that He was God. But a counterinfluence pressed in, and the evil angels were working through the congregation to raise doubts that would cause disbelief so that it would shut out every ray of light that God would permit to shine. No more could Christ do in such a place. You can see what a hold Satan had and what mistakes the people had made; they had not advanced, and because they had not advanced they had been working under the generalship of Satan and yet claimed that they were working under the generalship of God. But God had nothing to do with their unbelief and their rising up against Jesus Christ.

I wish you could see and feel that if you are not advancing you are retrograding. Satan understood this; he knew how to take advantage of the human mind, and he had taken advantage of the human family ever since they had first stood upon the field of battle against the powers of darkness. Christ knew what the warfare was to be.

Who was watching this warfare that was going on? Who was watching when Christ stood on the banks of Jordan and offered such a prayer as heaven had never listened to before, and a light like a dove broke forth

## Advancing in Christian Experience

from the heavens, and a voice was heard to say, "This is my beloved Son, in whom I am well pleased?" There were those who heard these things and spread the news everywhere among the Jews, and it went from one to the other, so this manifestation of God's power was not lost at that time.

What does that say to us? "This is my beloved Son, in whom I am well pleased." It says to you, I, God, have sent My Son into your world, and through Him is opened all heaven to fallen man. After the sin of Adam man was divorced from God, but Christ came in. He was represented through the sacrificial offerings until He came to our world. Here Christ offers this prayer, and what does it say to us? The human race is accepted in the Beloved. His long human arm encircles the race, while with His divine arm He grasps the throne of the Infinite, and He opens to man all of heaven. The gates are ajar today. Christ is in the heavenly sanctuary and your prayers can go up to the Father.

Christ says, If I go away, I will send you the Comforter, and when we have the Holy Spirit we have everything. We have knowledge, wisdom, power, and we have a connection with the God of wisdom. When heaven was opened to man, and God said, "This is my beloved Son, in whom I am well pleased," He said it to us. Your prayers, through faith in your substitute, Jesus Christ, are accepted. God accepts Christ, our substitute. He took human nature upon Himself and fought the battles that human nature is engaged in. He is connected with the divine and was to fight the battles with Satan.

Now, what we want you to see is the relation which you sustain to the work of God. What condescension God has shown that He should give His Son that we might defeat the powers of darkness! God was not the originator of sin, in order that He might rid the human race of sin. Here was the law of God, and He could not alter it a jot or tittle. It was a representation of His character. He could not change it because it is by that law that we are to be judged in the last day. It is no excuse to say that iniquity abounds, and that the law of God is done away or changed or altered. It is this that causes the existence of iniquity. This is the very work that Satan commenced in heaven, and he will carry it forward to the end. I ask you what position shall we take that we may be partakers of the divine nature? Why should we not see in that law the righteousness of Jesus Christ? Christ comes in and imputes to me His righteousness in His perfect obedience to that law.

Here the battle is before us. We see the battle, how Christ contended with the powers of darkness; and we see what He has done, and why the cross of Calvary had been erected between God and man. Then what? Man comes to Christ, and God and man are united at the cross, and here mercy and truth have met together, righteousness and truth have kissed each other. This is drawing man to the cross, where Christ died in behalf of man, to elevate the law of Jehovah, but not to lessen it one iota. Could He have done this, Christ need not have died. The cross of Calvary will stand in the judgment and testify to everyone the immutability and changeless character of the law of God, and not a word can be offered for sin in that day.

"And I, if I be lifted up from the earth, will draw all men unto me." What does that mean? The work must be carried on, and this little world was chosen in which to carry on this work. All the universe of heaven was interested in the great work. Every world that God has created is watching to see how the battle between the Lord of light and glory and the powers of darkness will end. Here is Satan, who has been seeking with all his power to shut out the true character of God, so that the world could not understand it, and under a garb of righteousness he works upon many who profess to be Christians, but they represent the character of Satan instead of the character of Jesus Christ. They misrepresent my Lord. They misrepresent the character of Jesus every time that they lack mercy, every time that they lack humility.

## Advancing in Christian Experience

Satan, by instigating in man a disposition to transgress the law of God, mystifies the character of God. Someone must come to vindicate the character of God, and here is Christ, who stands as the representation of the Father, and He is to work out the salvation of the human race.

That wonderful plan of salvation will bear investigation. All heaven is interested in this work. Up to the time when Christ died, though He was human, He was without sin, and He must bear His trials as a human being. There was to be no miracle interposed for Him. There had been miracles wrought for Him, as at the time the people were going to cast Him over the brow of the hill. Miracles have been wrought for men who have been followed by mobs, when the angel of the Lord would take their arms and protect the servants of God against the work of Satan.

I knew something of this in my early experience. I know whereof I am speaking. [The reporter indicates that here Ellen White related the experience of her husband when an angel walked with him through an angry mob. Recorded in *Life Sketches of James White and His Wife, Ellen G. White*, pp. 54, 55.]

All can testify that God has wrought in these cases; then just such things will take place with us as did with Christ. He was to work no miracle for Himself, but angels protected His life till the time came when He was to be betrayed by one of His disciples, till He was to give His life on Calvary's cross, and Satan stirred up the minds of men to think that the angels of heaven were indifferent. But every one was watching the contest with interest. From the moment that Christ knelt in prayer on the sod of Gethsemane till He died on the cross and cried out, "It is finished," the angels and all the universe of God looked on with the greatest interest. When those words were spoken, the plan was completed—the plan whereby Satan's power should be limited and broken, and whereby Christ should finally die. And when Christ rose from the dead His triumph was complete. Satan knew that his battle with Christ was lost, but yet he is at enmity with God.

It is man who has apostatized from God. Satan works on men's minds, trying to instill his devices into their minds and make them think that he is at last to be sovereign of this world. But not so, for the God of heaven lives and reigns, and has children on the earth that He will translate to heaven without their seeing death, when He shall come with power and great glory. We want to ask, What excuse have you when this has been done in your behalf? Just as soon as the trial was ended and Christ was hanging on the cross, Satan thought he had gained the victory; but as soon as Christ arose that thought was uprooted forever for every world that God had ever created. It was final. Never again could he have the least power over the worlds or in heaven.

The justice of God was seen in that He gave Christ to die to save man, for the law of condemned man to death; but the righteousness of Christ was brought in and imputed to him that he might be brought back to his loyalty to God. And when Christ's work was done, the news was heralded through the heavenly hosts.

When Jesus arose triumphant over the grave, and when He ascended from the Mount of Olives, He was not only in sight of a few disciples, but many were looking on. There was a multitude of angels, thousands upon thousands who beheld the Son of God as He ascended on high. And as He approached the city of God their voices were raised and the highest angels sang, "Lift up your heads, O ye gates; and be ye lift up, ye everlasting doors; and the King of glory shall come in." The question arises, "Who is this King of glory?" Then the answer comes back, "The Lord of hosts, he is the King of glory." Then the gates are thrown back and the heavenly train enters in, and the angels would bow in adoration before the Son of God, but He waves them back. Not yet; He must first hear from the Father that the sacrifice has been accepted, and He says, I have a

## Advancing in Christian Experience

request. What is that request? That those whom Thou hast given Me be with Me where I am. Then comes the answer, Let all the angels worship Him; and they bow in adoration before Him, and they touch their golden harps, and raise their voices in praise, saying, Worthy is the Lamb that was slain, and lives again, a conqueror. And how the arches of heaven ring with rejoicing!

Now Christ is in the heavenly sanctuary. And what is He doing? Making atonement for us, cleansing the sanctuary from the sins of the people. Then we must enter by faith into the sanctuary with Him, we must commence the work in the sanctuary of our souls. We are to cleanse ourselves from all defilement. We must "cleanse ourselves from all filthiness of the flesh and spirit, perfecting holiness in the fear of God." Satan will come and tempt you and you will give way to his temptations. What then? Why, come and humble your hearts in confession, and by faith grasp the arm of Christ in the heavenly sanctuary. Believe that Christ will take your confession and hold up His hands before the Father—hands that have been bruised and wounded in our behalf—and He will make an atonement for all who will come with confession. What if you cannot understand about this matter? He says, "He that lacketh these things is blind, and cannot see afar off, and hath forgotten that he was purged from his old sins" (2 Peter 1:19).

Now brethren and sisters, I want you to see that you must add to your faith virtue; and to virtue knowledge; and to knowledge temperance; and to temperance patience; and to patience godliness; and to godliness brotherly kindness; and to brotherly kindness charity. For if these things be in you, and abound, they make you that ye shall neither be barren nor unfruitful in the knowledge of our Lord Jesus Christ.

Now when you commence to work, Satan is going to work in an opposite direction; and if you are unkind and harsh, and if you are not seen in the house of God bearing your cross, you have not the knowledge of the Lord Jesus Christ; you do not discern Him in His love and matchless purity.

Many will say, I am saved, I am saved, I am saved. Well, have they been cleansed from all filthiness of the flesh and spirit? And can they cleanse themselves by the righteousness of the law? Jesus Christ came to this world, and there is His righteousness to impart to the children of men who are obeying the law of God. The whole world can say, I am saved, as well as any transgressor today. They can say, I believe on Christ that He is my Saviour, but why do they disregard His law which is the transcript of His character? When they disregard the law of Jehovah they disregard the Lord Jesus Christ.

Now, I want to say to you before closing, that we have a wonderful friend in Jesus, who came to save His people from the transgression of the law. What is sin? The only definition of sin is that it is the transgression of the law. Then here is Jesus Christ, who comes right in and imparts His righteousness to us; we cannot overcome in our own strength, but by faith in Him. If you will believe [in] Jesus Christ, you will have Him today. You must believe that He is your Saviour now, and that He imputes to you His righteousness because He has died, and because He has been obedient unto every requirement of that transgressed law of God. If you do this, you will have a saving knowledge of Jesus Christ. Adam and Eve lost Eden because they transgressed that law, but you will lose heaven if you transgress it.

We can be filled with all the fullness of God. Our lives may measure with the life of God. Then can we press back the powers of darkness. Glory to God in the highest! I love Him because He first loved me. I will magnify His name. I rejoice in His love, and when we shall enter in through the gates into the city it will be the highest privilege to cast my crown at His feet. Why? Because He gave me the victory, because He wrought out the plan of salvation. And when I look at the glory, and at the saints redeemed, just like a flash will I cast my crown at the feet of my Redeemer. It is His; it was He who purchased my redemption. Glory to God in the highest! Let us praise Him and talk of His mightiness and of what He will do for us. Let us keep His law and then He can trust us, for He has a law and He will reward obedience to that law; He will give us a crown of glory.

Now, brethren, we are almost home; we shall soon hear the voice of the Saviour richer than any music, saying, Your warfare is accomplished. Enter into the joy of thy Lord. Blessed, blessed, benediction; I want to hear it from His immortal lips. I want to praise Him; I want to honor Him that sitteth on the throne. I want my voice to echo and re-echo through the courts of heaven. Will you be there? Then you must educate your voice to praise Him on earth, and then you can join the heavenly choir and sing the song of Moses and the Lamb. God help us, and fill us with all fullness and power, and then we can taste of the joys of the world to come.

# A Chosen People

*Sermon, Oct. 21, 1888, MS 17, 1888*

"Ye are a chosen generation, a royal priesthood, an holy nation, a peculiar people; that ye should shew forth the praises of him who hath called you out of darkness into his marvelous light...Dearly beloved, I beseech you as strangers and pilgrims, abstain from fleshy lusts, which war against the soul; having your conversation honest among the Gentiles: that, whereas they speak against you as evildoers, they may by your good works, which they shall behold, glorify God in the day of visitation" (1 Peter 2:9–12).

These words point out the high standard that we should maintain before the world. The God of heaven has done everything that He could do to win our allegiance. He made an infinite sacrifice that we might be brought out of darkness into His marvelous light.

Claiming possession of the world, Satan determined to get possession also of the minds of men. He comes to them with the advantages offered by the world, and says, "All these shall be yours if you will worship me." And many, lured on by the prize held out by him, bow at his shrine.

With a mighty arm and with wonderful manifestations of His power, God brought Israel out of Egypt. He made them His chosen people, and gave them His law. He said to them: "Thou art an holy people unto the Lord thy God.... Know therefore that the Lord thy God, he is God, the faithful God, which keepeth covenant and mercy with them that love him and keep his commandments to a thousand generations" (Deut. 7:6–9).

To us also have been spoken the words, "Ye are a chosen nation." Our work is to show forth the praises of Him who hath called us out of darkness into His marvelous light. How are we to do this? By showing to the world that we are a commandment-keeping people, walking in harmony with God's law. By never losing sight of His goodness and love, and by making everything in our lives subordinate to the claims of His Word. Thus we shall be representatives of Christ, showing forth in our lives a transcript of His character.

"But," one says, "I thought the commandments were a yoke of bondage." It is those only who break the law that find it a yoke of bondage. To those who keep the law it is life and joy and peace and happiness. The law is a mirror, into which we may look and discern the defects in our characters. Should we not be grateful that God has provided a means whereby we may discover our shortcomings?

There is no power in the law to save or to pardon the transgressor. What, then, does it do? It brings the repentant sinner to Christ. Paul declares, "I... have taught you publicly, and from house to house, testifying to the Jews, and also to the Greeks, repentance toward God and faith toward our Lord Jesus Christ" (Acts 20:20, 21). Why did he preach repentance? Because the law of God had been transgressed. Those who have broken the law must repent. Why did he preach faith in Christ? Because Christ is the One who has redeemed sinners from the penalty of the law. The law points to the remedy for sin—repentance toward God and faith in Christ.

Do you wonder that Satan wants to get rid of the law? He and all his agencies are striving to trample underfoot the commandments of Jehovah, and to erect a standard of their own. We are to show that God's chosen people will keep His commandments, refusing to swerve to the right or to the left in disobedience. They are to show that the truth of heavenly origin has done great things for them, that its converting power has taken hold of their souls.

Paul declares, "I had not known sin, but by the law...I was alive without the law once: but when the commandment came, sin revived, and I died" (Rom. 7:7–9). The commandments remained the same, but Paul died.

In true conversion, the sinner is first convicted of his real condition. He realizes that he is a transgressor of God's law, and that the Lord has claims upon him which He will not relinquish. He sees that the connection between himself and God has been broken, but that if he repents of his transgression, confesses his sin, and takes hold by faith upon the grace of Christ, the connection that has been broken will be restored.

If God could have changed His law to meet man in his fallen condition, Christ need not have come to this world. Because the law was immutable, unchangeable, God sent His only-begotten Son to die for the fallen race. But did the Saviour take upon Himself the guilt of human beings and impute to them His righteousness in order that they might continue to violate the precepts of Jehovah? No, no! Christ came because there was no possibility of man's keeping the law in his own strength. He came to bring him strength to obey the precepts of the law. And the sinner, repenting of his transgression, may come to God and say, "O Father, I plead forgiveness through the merits of a crucified and risen Saviour." God will accept all who come to Him in the name of Jesus.

My object in speaking these words to you today is to lead you to take your minds off the things of this world, and place them on the things of eternity. If your affections are set on things above, if in the daily life you are seeking to follow the perfect pattern, you need never be discouraged. The enemy may seek to cast his dark shadow between you and Christ, but your faith is to pierce the gloom. What are we in this world for? To represent Christ and to be a blessing to our fellow men. Christ is to be formed in us, the hope of glory. We are to live His life, that our lives may show forth to the world the love of God and the power of the gospel.

When God's people take their eyes off the things of this world, and place them on heaven and heavenly things, they will be a peculiar people, because they will see the mercy and goodness and compassion that God has shown to the children of men. His love will call forth a response from them, and their lives will show to those around them that the Spirit of God is controlling them, that they are setting their affections on things above, not on the things of the earth.

In thinking of heaven we may put our imagination to the utmost stretch, and think the loftiest thoughts that we are capable of thinking, and our minds will grow weary in the effort to comprehend the breadth and depth and height of the subject. It is impossible for our minds to take in the great themes of eternity. It is impossible for us even to make an effort to understand these things without the effort affecting our whole character for good, and having an uplifting influence on our minds. As we think of how Christ came to our world to die for fallen man, we understand something of the price that was paid for our redemption, and we realize that there is no true goodness or greatness apart from God.

Only by the light shining from the cross of Calvary can we know to what depths of sin and degradation the human race has fallen through sin. Only by the length of the chain let down from heaven to draw us up can we know the depths to which we had sunk. And it is only by keeping the unseen [realities] in view that we can understand anything of the wonderful theme of redemption.

## Counsels to Ministers

*Discourse to Ministers, Oct. 21, 1888, MS 8a, 1888*

"I am the true vine, and my Father is the husband-man. Every branch in me that beareth not fruit he taketh away: and every branch that beareth fruit, he purgeth it, that it may bring forth more fruit. Now ye are clean through the word which I have spoken unto you. Abide in me, and I in you. As the branch cannot bear fruit of itself, except it abide in the vine, no more can ye, except ye abide in me. I am the vine, ye are the branches: He that abideth in me, and I in him, the same bringeth forth much fruit: for without me ye can do nothing. If a man abide not in me, he is cast forth as a branch, and is withered; and men gather them, and cast them into the fire, and they are burned. If ye abide in me, and my words abide in you, ye shall ask what ye will, and it shall be done unto you. Herein is my Father glorified, that ye bear much fruit; so shall ye be my disciples."

Brethren, I want to ask you a question. How can we come to God with full assurance of faith if we bear no fruit that testifies to a change wrought in us by the grace of God, no fruit that shows that we are in fellowship with Christ? How can we approach God in faith and be abiding in Christ and He in us when by our works we show that we are not bearing fruit?

What is the fruit we should bear? The fruit of kindly words and deeds. In God's Word we are told what are the works of the flesh and what the fruits of the Spirit. "The works of the flesh are manifest, which are these, adultery, fornication, uncleanness, lasciviousness, idolatry, witchcraft, hatred, variance, emulations, wrath, strife, seditions, heresies, envyings, murders, drunkenness, revellings, and such like: of the which I tell you before, as I have also told you in time past, that they which do these things shall not inherit the kingdom of God. But the fruit of the Spirit is love, joy, peace, longsuffering, gentleness, goodness, faith, meekness, temperance: against such there is no law." Is not this sufficiently plain? None of us need walk in uncertainty. "And they that are Christ's have crucified the flesh with the affections and lusts. If we live in the Spirit, let us also walk in the Spirit. Let us not be desirous of vainglory, provoking one another, envying one another."

In order to have true spiritual discernment, in order to be conscious of our own weakness and deficiency and our unlikeness to Christ, we need a close connection with God. Then we shall have a humble opinion of ourselves. We shall be meek and lowly in heart, walking prayerfully and carefully before God. We shall not boast ourselves beyond our measure.

In every age the gospel ministry has tended to the same end. But every minute specification is not revealed in the Word of God. He desires us to use our reason and experience, by their help adopting methods and plans which, under the existing circumstances, are for the benefit of the church and the schools and the other institutions which have been established. "By their fruits ye shall know them." If erroneous opinions are entertained, search the Scriptures with hearts which are humbled before God. Pray to the Lord, believing that He hears, and that He is a rewarder of those who diligently seek Him. If we will only believe, we shall receive the help we need.

The message "Go forward" is still to be heard and respected. The varying circumstances taking place in our world call for labor which will meet these peculiar developments. The Lord has need of men who are spiritually sharp and clear-sighted, men worked by the Holy Spirit, who are certainly receiving manna fresh from heaven. Upon the minds of such, God's Word flashes light, revealing to them more than ever before the safe path. The Holy Spirit works upon mind and heart. The time has come when through God's messengers the scroll is being unrolled to the world. Instructors in our schools should never be bound about by being told that they are to teach only what has been taught hitherto. Away with these restrictions. There is a God to give the message His people shall speak. Let not any minister feel under bonds or be gauged by men's measurement. The gospel must be fulfilled in accordance with the messages God sends. That which God gives His servants to speak today would not perhaps have been present truth twenty years ago, but it is God's message for this time.

"Let no man deceive himself. If any man among you seemeth to be wise in this world, let him become a fool"—in his own estimation —"that he may be wise." An experience of this kind is needed here, right with the men who have been forward to speak in this meeting. "For the wisdom of this world is foolishness with God. For it is written, He taketh the wise in their own craftiness. And again, The Lord knoweth the thoughts of the wise, that they are vain. Therefore let no man glory in men." Do consider this, I beseech you. "Thus saith the Lord, Let not the wise man glory in his wisdom, neither let the mighty man glory in his might, let not the rich man glory in his riches: but let him that glorieth glory in this, that he understandeth and knoweth me, that I am the Lord which exercise lovingkindness, judgment, and righteousness in the earth; for in these things I delight, saith the Lord."

Let men and women who are truly converted offer themselves in all humility to the service of the Lord, for verily He hath need of them. First, they must be emptied of all selfishness. They will be cleansed vessels unto honor. They will reflect the bright beams of the [Son] of Righteousness to all with whom they come in contact. Partakers of the divine nature, they will be savors of life unto life. They will not talk of the faults of others, but will repeat the words of divine wisdom which have penetrated and illuminated their hearts. They will be men who fear to talk and make sport of God's messengers, but men who pray much.

"Where the Spirit of the Lord is, there is liberty. But we all, with open face beholding as in a glass the glory of the Lord, are changed into the same image from glory to glory, even as by the Spirit of the Lord." John declares, "That which was from the beginning, which we have heard, which we have seen with our eyes, which we have looked upon, and our hands have handled, of the Word of life;...that which we have seen and heard declare we unto you, that ye also may have fellowship with us; and truly our fellowship is with the Father, and with his Son Jesus Christ."

As John studied the life of Christ in the Word, he beheld as in a glass the glory of the Lord, and he became changed into the same image, from glory to glory, from character to character, till he was like that which he adored. He imitated the life in which he delighted. He knew the Saviour by an experimental knowledge. His Master's lessons were engraved on his soul. When he testified of the Saviour's grace, the simplicity of his language was eloquent with the love that pervaded his whole being. He had not a doubt nor a suspicion. He entered into no controversy, no wearisome contention.

In witnessing for Christ he declared what he knew, what he had seen and heard. There was no supposition, no guesswork, about what he said. And when insult was put upon Christ, when He was slighted, John felt the slight to the very depths of his being, and broke forth into indignation which was a manifestation of his love for Jesus. Christ had humbled Himself; He had taken man's nature; and few could see Him as John saw Him. But John had an advanced experience; the darkness had passed away. On him the true light was shining, and in his epistles he breaks forth against sin, presenting Christ as the One who could cleanse from all iniquity.

It was John's deep love for Christ that led him to desire always to be close by His side, and this position was awarded him. Jesus loves those who represent the Father, and John could talk of this love as no other of the disciples could. He reveals to his fellow men that which he knows by living experience it is his duty to reveal, representing in his character the character of Christ. The glory of the Lord was expressed in his face. The beauty of holiness which had transformed him shone with a Christlike radiance from his countenance.

Those who truly love God must manifest loving-kindness of heart, judgment, and righteousness to all with whom they come in contact; for these are the works of God. There is nothing Christ needs so much as agents who feel the necessity of representing Him. Evil speaking and evil thinking are ruinous to the soul. This has been current in this conference. There is nothing the church lacks so much as the manifestation of Christlike love. As the members of the church unite together in sanctified association, cooperating with Christ, He lives and works in them. Our eyes need the anointing with the heavenly eyesalve, that we may see what we are, and what we ought to be, and that power is provided in Christ sufficient to enable us to reach the high standard of Christian perfection.

We must keep Jesus our pattern ever before us. This is and ever will be present truth. It was by beholding Jesus and appreciating the virtues of His character that John became one with his Master in spirit. With spiritual vision he saw Christ's glory, the glory as of the only begotten of the Father, full of grace and truth; and he was changed from glory to glory into His likeness. And to him was committed the work of telling of the Saviour's love and the love His children should manifest for one another. "This is the message that ye heard from the beginning," he writes, "that we should love one another.... We know that we have passed from death unto life, because we love the brethren. He that loveth not his brother abideth in death. Whosoever hateth his brother is a murderer: and ye know that no murderer hath eternal life abiding in him. Hereby perceive we the love of God, because he laid down his life for us: and we ought to lay down our lives for the brethren. But whoso hath this world's good, and seeth his brother have need, and shutteth up his bowels of compassion from him, how dwelleth the love of God in him? My little children, let us not love in word, neither in tongue; but in deed and in truth."

"Beloved, let us love one another: for love is of God; and every one that loveth is born of God, and knoweth God. He that loveth not knoweth not God; for God is love. In this was manifested the love of God toward us, because that God sent his only-begotten Son into the world, that we might live through him.... Beloved, if God so loved us, we ought also to love one another.... God is love; and he that dwelleth in love dwelleth in God, and God in him."

But although John dwells so particularly on love, he does not clasp hands with sin. Hear his words regarding the apostate from the faith, he who has had a knowledge of the truth but has departed from the faith, giving heed to seducing spirits. "Whosoever transgresseth, and abideth not in the doctrine of Christ, hath not God. He that abideth in the doctrine of Christ, he hath both the Father and the Son. If there come any unto you, and bring not this doctrine, receive him not into your house, neither bid him God speed: for he that biddeth him Godspeed is partaker of his evil deeds." Let all consider this.

John writes further, "He that saith, I know him, and keepeth not his commandments, is a liar, and the truth is not in him. But whoso keepeth his word, in him verily is the love of God perfected .... He that saith he abideth in him ought himself also so to walk, even as he walked."

The Lord has plain words for those who, like the Pharisees, make great boast of their piety but whose hearts are destitute of the love of God. The Pharisees refused to know God and Jesus Christ whom He had sent. Are we not in danger of doing the same thing as did the Pharisees and scribes?

But while reproof is to be given, it must be given in accordance with Christ's direction. The apostle Paul writes, "Brethren, if a man be overtaken in a fault, ye which are spiritual, restore such an one in the spirit of meekness; considering thyself, lest thou also be tempted." This work is given not only to Ministers but to every individual member of the church. It is to be carried out in the family and in the church. Love and unity strengthen by exercise. Do not become impatient with your brother's faults and weaknesses. On another point you may well be disgusted with your own weakness. We are related to one another in the mysterious web of humanity. We are but threads which help to compose the great whole.

We see individuals committing errors, and we are pained because their lives are not in accordance with the Bible standard of righteousness. But we are not to become impatient. If we have the mind of Christ, we shall feel a burden for the welfare of him who has forgotten to be a doer of the Word. Do not speak of his errors to others. Follow the rule Jesus has given. Go to the wrongdoer alone first, and see if by words of wisdom you cannot save him.

The apostle James, inspired by Jesus Christ, lays down our duty in clear lines. "Brethren, if any of you do err from the truth, and one convert him; let him know, that he which converteth the sinner from the error of his way, shall save a soul from death, and shall hide a multitude of sins." We are Christ's witnesses, Christ's representatives. In his epistle to Titus, Paul charges him to set in order things that are wanting in the church. "Speak thou the things which become sound doctrine," he says. The teacher of truth is to educate all, both old and young. He is to exhort aged men to be "sober, grave, temperate, sound in faith, in charity, in patience. The aged women likewise, that they be in behaviour as becometh holiness, not false accusers, not given to much wine, teachers of good things; that they may teach the young women to be sober, to love their husbands, to love their children, to be discreet, chaste, keepers at home, good, obedient to their own husbands, that the word of God be not blasphemed." When those who profess to be servants of Christ do not walk circumspectly, God is dishonored and the truth is reproached.

"Young men likewise exhort to be sober minded. In all things shewing thyself a pattern of good works: in doctrine shewing uncorruptness, gravity, sincerity, sound speech, that cannot be condemned; that he that is of the contrary part may be ashamed, having no evil thing to say of you."

I have been pained to hear so much jesting and joking among old and young as they are seated at the dining table. I have inquired, Are these men aware that there is by their side a Watcher who is disgusted with their spirit and the influence which they exert, and is making a record of their words and actions? Will our Ministers, young and old, countenance these things? Shall not we who name the name of Christ take heed to the words, "*In all things* shewing thyself a pattern of good works, in doctrine shewing uncorruptness, gravity, sincerity, sound speech, that cannot be condemned"? If the truth as it is in Jesus abides in our hearts, it will sanctify our lives. Our speech will not be evil. Obeying the truth we shall work the works of righteousness.

By our words and deeds we may reveal the power of the truth to transform the character. We may each reveal that we depend on Christ's righteousness, not upon our own manufactured righteousness. We may abide in Christ as the branch abides in the vine, having such a living connection with Him that it is a pleasure to work as He worked, to be a help and blessing to our brethren. We can work the works of Christ, doing those things that are pleasing in His sight.

In all you do, make Christ the center of attraction. Constantly look to Him who is your pattern, the Author and Finisher of your faith. Cultivate constant, fervent gratitude to God for the gift of His beloved Son. Represent Christ. Squander not your moral forces upon trifles, but earnestly improve the opportunities given you to reflect the light of the Sun of Righteousness. Cease to glorify man. Glory in Christ and the truth. You may crown Jesus with honor, for though so meek and lowly He was a daily conqueror over temptation. Every soul who is a partaker of the divine nature is an overcomer in His own behalf, and is victorious, having escaped the corruption that is in the world through lust.

We are laborers together with God; and not only are we to have respect unto the recompense of reward, but we are to labor zealously for the Redeemer's glory by bringing sheaves to the Master. Every soul saved will swell the triumphant anthems of praise which the redeemed will sing. In every fellow being we are to see the purchase of the blood of Christ. The Saviour's interest is identified with the interests of the souls He has ransomed by an infinite sacrifice.

My brethren and sisters, do we realize the importance of this subject? Why are we so listless? Why are we satisfied to remain so poorly fitted to work for the uplifting of humanity? Why is not every entrusted capability used for the Master? Why are so many contented with the feeble, lifeless condition of our churches? The heavenly universe is looking with amazement upon our Christless work. Neglect is seen in all our borders. Slipshod work is tolerated and passed by. How long shall this continue? Shall we not arise, and with determined, harmonious effort take up our responsibilities, laboring in Christ's lines with sanctified capabilities? Put away the controversial spirit which you have been educating yourselves in for years. Educate yourselves to pray to God in sincerity and truth. Sing with the spirit and understanding also. Much is expected of us.

What are our young men doing? Jesus is waiting to bind their hearts up with His great heart of love, to bind their interests with His own. He says to them, Young men, flee youthful lusts. Will you obey His voice? You are surely not doing this now. The truth is an inherent power, and if brought into the sanctuary of the soul, will draw men and women to Christ. It will win its way to human hearts. To those who look to Him Christ by His Holy Spirit reveals the beauty of truth. He shows Himself to be the sin-pardoning Saviour.

Young men, you may have the truth on your side. When your heart and all your faculties are brought under the influence of truth, when you bring the truth, with all its living, sanctifying principles, into your heart, you will have confidence to present it to others. Christ is then made unto you wisdom, and righteousness, and sanctification, and redemption. We are laborers together with God, and Christ is by your side. You are yoked up with Him, He leading and guiding. Such a worker is as a sharp sickle in the harvest field. He does not use his God-given powers in debating. That is Satan's line. Pointing to the cross of Calvary, he cries, "Behold the Lamb of God, which taketh away the sin of the world." He urges sinners to behold eternal realities. He holds the telescope before his eyes, that by faith he may discern these realities. Like Moses, he endures the seeing of Him who is invisible. He does not seek ease or amusement. He does not visit the churches to be petted and waited upon, to jest and joke. He knows that there is stern, earnest work to be done. Those who are truly converted do not waste the precious moments in foolish conversation and making a mock of their brethren. By words that have a weight of influence for good they give full proof of their ministry. They deny self and lift the cross, and follow Jesus the crossbearer. They ardently desire to yoke up with Christ, to lift His burdens and partake of His sufferings.

Young men, Jesus calls you, saying, "Follow Me." Those who follow Him will not walk in darkness, for Christ is the light of life. Our older ministering brethren must drop some of their responsibilities or else they will go down in the silence of the grave. The aged standard-bearers may act as worthy counselors and living witnesses, but their younger and stronger brethren should bear the heavy burdens. John says, "I have written unto you, young men, because ye are strong,...and ye have overcome the wicked one." You whose eyes are not dimmed, whose brain power has not been worn by constant taxation, should plan, devise, and execute, treating the aged workers with tenderness, as fathers, and looking up to them as counselors and guides. Young workers should respect the age and experience of their older brethren.

The Lord desires us all to be learners in the school of Christ. Young and old have precious lessons to learn from the divine Teacher, and when these lessons are learned they are to impart them to others. God is presenting to the minds of men divinely appointed precious gems of truth, appropriate for our time. God has rescued these truths from the companionship of error, and has placed them in their proper framework. When these truths are given their rightful position in God's great plan, when they are presented intelligently and earnestly, and with reverential awe, by the Lord's servants, many will conscientiously believe because of the weight of evidence, without waiting for every supposed difficulty which may suggest itself to their minds to be removed. Others, not discerning spiritual things, will keep themselves in a combative frame of mind, opposing every argument that does not meet their ideas. Shall this miserable work cease?

Those who have not been sinking the shaft deeper and still deeper into the mine of truth will see no beauty in the precious things presented at this conference. When the will is once set in stubborn opposition to the light given, it is difficult to yield, even under the convincing evidence which has been in this conference. To controvert, to question, to criticize, to ridicule, is the education many have received and the fruit they bear. They refuse to admit evidence. The natural heart is in warfare against light, truth, and knowledge. Jesus Christ has been in every sleeping room where you have been entertained. How many prayers went up to heaven from these rooms?

Satan is fruitful in bringing up devices to evade the truth. But I call upon you to believe the words I speak today. Truth of heavenly origin is confronting Satan's falsehoods, and this truth will prevail. We do well to remember that Christ is the light of the world, and that fresh beams of light are constantly reflected from the Source of all light.

He who studies the truth, who prayerfully opens the eyes of his understanding to see and his heart to receive the bright beams of the Sun of Righteousness, will be in harmony with the messenger and the message God sends. All the opposition, all the prejudice, all the suggestions of the enemy, will never make the truth less precious or less true. Only when men yield to the [subtlety] of the enemy does the truth become darkness to them. But even though the truth is opposed and spoken against by those who should be blessed, strengthened, and made joyful by it, its value and brightness is not lessened; for the Lord's messengers will hold up the telescope to the spiritual eye, that the truth may be seen from all points, and its value appreciated.

A fair investigation will not fail to reveal wonderful things in God's Word. Every jot of resistance places the opposer in a darker shade. He does not want to see. He will not search God's Word. But opposition and resistance only serve to bring out truth in new, distinct lines. The more truth is spoken against, the brighter it will shine. Thus the precious ore is polished. Every word of slander spoken against it, every misrepresentation of its value, awakens attention and is the means of leading to closer investigation as to what is saving truth. The truth becomes more highly estimated. New beauty and greater value are revealed from every point of view.

Brethren, God has most precious light for His people. I call it not new light; but O, it is strangely new to many. Jesus said to His disciples, "A new commandment I give unto you, That ye love one another; as I have loved you." This was really an old commandment, which had been given in the Old Testament scriptures, but it had been lost. It had not been practiced. The command that they should love one another as Christ had loved them was indeed new to the disciples. But the revealing of this love would give to the world an unmistakable evidence that they were God's children.

I call upon the young men who are entering the work as Ministers to take heed how they hear. Be careful how you oppose the precious truths of which you now have so little knowledge. Search the Scriptures for yourselves. You have altogether too limited knowledge of yourself. Know for yourselves what is truth. Do not take any man's words, any man's prejudices, any man's arguments, any man's theories. This has been done by Ministers to the injury of their experience, and it has left them novices when they should be wise in the Scriptures and in the power of God. Take your Bibles, humble yourselves, and weep and fast and pray before the Lord, as did Nathanael, seeking to know the truth. Jesus' divine eye saw Nathanael praying, and answered his prayer.

I saw an angel of God inquiring of these men who have educated themselves as debaters, "How many prayers have you offered?" Oh, your levity, your speeches, are all written in the book. If you only knew how Christ has regarded your religious attitude at this meeting!

You must gain an experience for yourselves. I beg of you not to think that long sermons are an unmistakable evidence of your ministerial ability. Oh, there is something more to the ministry than sermonizing. Many, many discourses, like the offering of Cain, are profitless because Christless. Those who give them tire the people and fail to give them proper spiritual food.

Piety must be practiced in the home. Interested personal efforts must be made for those around you. Seek the Lord in private prayer. Ask Christ to do for you what you need to have done. He has been tempted in all points like as we are, and He knows how to succor those that are tempted. God calls upon you to leave the atmosphere of unbelief in which you have been dwelling, and place yourselves in an atmosphere of faith and confidence. Do your best. Do not seek wisdom from finite men, who may be bewildered by the temptations of Satan, who may plant the seeds of doubt rather than the seeds of faith. Go to Jesus, "who giveth to all men liberally, and upbraideth not." Has not His invitation reached your ears and touched your heart? He says, "Come unto me, all ye that [labor] and are heavy laden, and I will give you rest. Take my yoke upon you, and learn of me; for I am meek and lowly in heart: and ye shall find rest unto your souls. For my yoke is easy, and my burden [is] light."

Let no human hand place a yoke upon your neck. Take the yoke Christ gives. Learn of Him; for He is meek and lowly, and you will find rest. It is Christ's meekness and lowliness that you need. Go to the Lord with the faith, simplicity, and confidence of a little child. Tell Him the whole trouble, withholding nothing. Ask Him to teach you how to use your entrusted talents in the best way. Thus you may increase your talents. If you go out to labor in any portion of the Lord's great moral vineyard, take heed; keep watch over yourself, over your thoughts and words. Pray for an understanding heart, for a knowledge of how to humble yourself before the Lord. Ask for Christ's grace and efficiency, and you will not be left to labor alone. God gives every humble, devoted learner a clearer insight into the truth. He will give them precious souls as their hire.

I have been instructed that many go forth to preach who do not know how to labor for the salvation of sinners. They are not themselves consecrated to God. They need to be converted. Many have been dedicated to the sacred work of the ministry when, if close examination were made in regard to their religious experience, it would be seen that they need to seek most earnestly for the transforming grace of Jesus Christ before they can teach sinners how to seek in faith for pardon.

Those who would be laborers together with God must receive wisdom from the Great Teacher who is our example in all things, in order to present the truth in its simplicity. Learn of Christ. All pride, all selfishness, all self-importance, must be cut away from all teachers. All the *sang-froid,* which is so common, the theatrical gestures, all lightness and trifling, all jesting and joking, must be seen by the one who wears Christ's yoke to be "not convenient"—an offense to God and a denial of Christ. It unfits the mind for solid thought and solid labor. It makes men inefficient, superficial, and spiritually diseased.

He who believes the truth for this time will practice personal piety. The language of his heart will be, "Who is sufficient for these things?" Let every minister be sedate. As he studies the life of Christ he will see the necessity of walking circumspectly. Yet he may be, and will be, if connected with the [Son] of Righteousness, cheerful and happy, showing forth the praises of Him who hath called him out of darkness into His marvelous light. The conversation will be pure, entirely free from all slang phrases.

If Christ is abiding in your heart, you will show meekness and gentleness and purity of thought. You will follow elevated, noble principles, because you have learned the lessons taught in the school of Christ. If you have not felt the need of learning every day in this school, it is time you did feel this need. Learn of Christ, and then go forth in the strength of Him who has said, "Lo, I am with you always, even unto the end of the world." A divided heart God will not accept. Put your whole soul into your work, and never leave your work half done because you wish to go to another place. God will accept only faithful work. Reprove, rebuke, exhort, with all long-suffering and doctrine. Bind off your work thoroughly. Leave no dropped stitches for someone else to pick up. Do not disappoint Christ. Determine that you will succeed, and in the strength of Christ you may give full proof of your ministry.

A minister is one who Ministers. If you confine your work to sermonizing, the flock of God will suffer; for they need personal effort. Let your discourses be short. Long sermons wear out both you and the people. If Ministers would make their sermons only half as long, they would do more good and would have strength left for personal work. Visit families, pray with them, converse with them, search the Scriptures with them, and you will do them good. Give them evidence that you seek their prosperity, and want them to be healthy Christians. If you are staying in a family, do not allow yourself to be waited on. Show that you wish to be helpful. If possible, use the ax or the hoe. Bring in water and wood. Show that you regard work as a blessing. Physical exercise will be a blessing to you, and will increase your influence for good. Remember that to minister means far more than merely preaching.

Nothing is so discouraging to the advancement of present truth as the haphazard work done by some of the Ministers for the churches. Faithful labor is needed. The churches are ready to die, because they are not strengthened in Christlikeness. The Lord is not pleased with the loose way in which the churches are left because men are not faithful stewards of God's grace. They do not receive His grace, and therefore cannot impart it. The churches are weak and sickly because of the unfaithfulness of those who are supposed to labor among them, whose duty it is to have an oversight over them, watching for souls as they that must give an account. Be thorough and determined in your efforts to serve God. Keep the eye fixed on Christ. Do not fix your attention on some favorite minister, copying his example and imitating his gestures; in short, becoming his shadow. Let no man put his mold upon you. Let the hand of God mold and fashion you after the divine similitude. Cease from man, whose breath is in his nostrils. Hang your helpless soul on Jesus Christ. He is unchangeable, the same yesterday, today, and forever.

My heart was made glad as I heard the testimonies borne after the discourse on Sabbath. These testimonies made no reference to the speaker, but to the light and truth; and this is the way it should ever be. Praise no man; flatter no man; and permit no man to praise or flatter you. Satan will do enough of this work. Lose sight of the instrument, and think of Jesus. Praise the Lord. Give glory to God. Make melody to God in your hearts. Talk of the truth. Talk of the Christian's hope, the Christian's heaven.

If we neglect to walk in the light given, it becomes darkness to us; and the darkness is proportionate to the light and privileges which we have not improved. Christ says, "If therefore the light that is in thee be darkness, how great is that darkness!" If we walk in the knowledge of the truth, our light will shine to those around us in spirit, in words, in actions; we will be fruitful branches of the living vine. If we know God's requirements and claim to love Him, yet cherish sin, God will not hear us when we ask for His blessing; for He does not minister to sin. There are those whose conscience is hardened by habitual sin. They bear no rich clusters of precious fruit, because they are not branches of the true vine. Their prayers rise no higher than their heads, because they are in their prayers presenting only a form of words, whether offered in the church, in the family, or in secret. They receive no strength, because they ask amiss.

But when those who are striving with all their power to overcome, confess their sins, God is faithful and just to forgive their sins, and to cleanse them from all unrighteousness for Christ's sake. When brought into the sanctuary of the soul, the truth of God works by faith and purifies the soul, elevating, refining, ennobling it.

There was a time when Israel could not prevail against their enemies. This was because of Achan's sin. God declared, "Neither will I be with you any more, except ye destroy the accursed thing from among you." God is the same today. If defiling sins are cherished by those who claim to believe the truth, the displeasure of God rests upon the church, and He will not remove it until the members do all in their power to show their hatred for sin, and their determination to cast it out of the church. God is displeased with those who call evil good and good evil. If jealousy, evil surmising, and evil-speaking are allowed to have a place in the church, that church is under the frown of God. It will be spiritually unhealthy until it is cleansed from these sins, for till then God cannot reveal His power to strengthen and elevate His people and give them victory.

God is not pleased with the slothful work done in the churches. He expects His stewards to be true and faithful in giving reproof and correction. They are to expel wrong after the rule God has given in His Word, not according to their own ideas and impulses. No harsh means must be used, no unfair, hasty, impulsive work done. The efforts made to cleanse the church from moral uncleanness must be made in God's way. There must be no partiality, no hypocrisy. There must be no favorites, whose sins are regarded as less sinful than those of others. Oh, how much we all need the baptism of the Holy Ghost. Then we shall always work with the mind of Christ, with kindness, compassion, and sympathy, showing love for the sinner while hating sin with a perfect hatred.

A work needs to be done for many who are assembled here. The door of the heart is blocked up with the rubbish of selfishness, questioning, criticism, judgment pronounced in accordance with the unsanctified heart. Now is the time to seek God, with earnest confession and contrition, that He may turn His face toward us, and light and blessing come into our midst. Then the enemy will be disappointed. The heavenly universe will rejoice, and souls who are now under temptation and the frown of God will be won to Christ. Shall we not clear away the darkness by doing the work God has given us to do? We are laborers together with God. Jesus is waiting to work in us and by us and through us to will and to do of His good pleasure. If we neglect the Lord's heritage and feel little burden for the church and souls perishing in their sins, we are condemned by God for not strengthening that which was ready to die. If, as Christ's overseers, we do our work with an eye single to the glory of God, there is no reason why the church should be weak, faithless, and corrupt. Let the watchmen on the walls of Zion awake! Let them do their duty with fidelity. They need so much the heavenly endowment, that they may be laborers together with God in the great plan of salvation. To those who have been true and faithful Christ will say, "Come, ye blessed of my Father, inherit the kingdom prepared for you from the foundation of the world." "Enter thou into the joy of thy Lord." All who enter the kingdom of heaven as conquerors will understand the meaning of this benediction, for they will have done the work Christ has given them to do. They have participated with Him in saving the souls of their fellow men. Through the grace of Christ they have brought sheaves to the Master, and with all the heavenly universe they rejoice as they see souls that have been saved through their earnest efforts, given abundant entrance into heaven, made heirs of God and joint heirs with Christ. How foolish then will appear all fear and distrust of Christ, as the redeemed see that He was waiting to give them freely the richest blessings of heaven.

Let none here shut themselves away from God by their perversity of spirit, and then keep complaining that they have no light. Arise, dear souls; arise by faith, and do what you ought to do. Christ says, Follow Me, and you shall not walk in darkness. Let go your human wisdom, and ask God for that wisdom which is pure, elevating, and ennobling, and it shall be given you. Come up out of the cellar of doubt, of unbelief, of jealousy, and evil surmising, into the upper chamber of faith, hope, courage, and thankfulness. Make melody to God in the heart. The garden of the Lord is strewn with precious flowers. Gather the roses and the lilies and the pinks from God's spiritual garden. Rejoice in the Lord always, and again I say, Rejoice. Let not the world receive the impression that there is no peace nor joy nor happiness in serving the Lord.

It is Satan's work to misrepresent the Father and His Son, to misrepresent truth and gloss over error, making it appear as truth. But connected with God, we may distinguish between the genuine and the spurious. Light will dispel darkness. Why should we not avail ourselves of God's gracious promises, returning the glory to Him in heartfelt thanksgiving? Christ died for us that we might enter into possession of eternal riches. With hearts filled with gratitude to God, let us use the opportunities He has placed within our reach, that we may be fitted and prepared for the mansions Jesus has gone to prepare for those who love Him. If we fail through indolence, unbelief, worldliness, or covetousness, we shall suffer irreparable loss, for we shall lose an eternity of bliss. I tell you in the fear of God that day by day we are forming characters that will decide our destiny for weal or for woe.

Heaven is a holy place, and there entereth into it nothing that defileth. We cannot be truly happy here unless God's will is our will, unless we are sanctified to God, body, soul, and spirit. The more we think of heaven, the more happiness we shall have.

## Remarks on Missionary Work

*Oct. 23, 1888, MS 10, 1888*

Our Saviour has given to everyone his work, and no one of us can plead any excuse to God why he has not done the very work which God has given him to do. He does not require of the men to whom He has entrusted two talents the use of five talents; but He expects us to do our very best according to the capability and the powers which He has given us. And while we seek to put to use the talents He has given us, these talents will improve.

The plans which have been suggested by our brother we believe to be sound, and if we will practice something in this line in the several churches, we shall find that those churches which carry out a system of labor will be living churches; for a working church is a living church. But here comes in the difficulty. There needs to be ability to educate properly, to teach how the different members shall have their part in the work; and every one who is set as a leader in the church, or a minister who has charge in the churches should consider this a part of his work. Now how is it possible for them to neglect this part of the work, and yet to be able to fulfill the direction that is given in the Bible by Paul, to "present every man perfect in Christ Jesus?" This is the very work that is devolving on the teacher. It is to try to educate, educate, educate, by precept and example; and if we can get a church in working order, and if we can teach them how to work in this very line, you will find that these workers will have a special interest. "Why, yes," they will say, "I have acted a part in that work; I have done something in that, and I have an interest to do more." Just according to the several ability which God has committed to them can they work intelligently, and work in Christ.

Now here is the great essential point, to be sure that these workers have the spirit of Jesus Christ. If they are filled with the love of God, which should be in the heart of every worker, and if they seek wisdom from above, they will become more and more intelligent in regard to their work, and they will become more efficient in their work and will come up to be useful workers. Now, the very first thing is to have our hearts and minds and ways and manners so that they will not offend. We want to be such excellent representatives of the missionary cause that it shall stand as high as possible. Our brother was speaking in regard to commencing on the bottom round of the ladder. I believe this is the best way. It is not best for those uneducated to grasp at the top round of the ladder and think that they can do the work; but if they will be humble they will begin to gain an experience and have an aptitude for the work.

I want to know why, as Christians who profess to believe the most solemn truths that God ever gave to mortals, we should not have works to correspond to our faith. Christ has said, "Let your light so shine before men, that they may see your good works, and glorify your Father which is in heaven." That is the work we are to do, and God will help us by letting His light shine through us. We want to be the very best and most intelligent workers that there are anywhere.

We can see many of our sisters who know how to crochet fine articles for their houses. Now, what if they would spend their time in earnest prayer to God and the study of His Word that He would help them to have heavenly wisdom to know how to save the souls of those around them? It looks to me as though this kind of work is hay, wood, and stubble, of substances that are consumable and perishable; but the work that they might do in cleansing their own household and working for their neighbors would present lasting results of good. And if they were interested in this work they might be sowing seeds of truth. We must sow beside all waters, and we do not know which shall prosper, this or that. But the first work is a personal consecration to God.

I have seen ladies in England who would be riding in their carriages with their little dogs in their arms and the little blanket to put over them, and the houses that were built, beautiful and expensive. You ask what these houses are for, and the answer is, "For the hounds and dogs." But you can see the little children and women, miserable and poor, in the streets, destitute of clothing. Now, what sense is there in that? Do you think that work will be as far reaching as eternity? We do not want to misuse any of God's creatures, but we want to give our first attention to those souls for whom Christ died, and we do not want to devote our means in such foolish channels. We do not want our means to flow out for our own selfish interests; but we want to use it in gaining that experience that will help us to advance the missionary work; and in doing this we are laying up a treasure in heaven. God Himself will connect with every self-sacrificing work and effort that shall be made to educate and train ourselves for labor, and will put His seal and mold on it. It may look to us very feeble, and we may never understand the results of our labor, but God knows all about it, and we sow beside all waters, not knowing which will prosper, this or that.

There are churches in different places which we may find that are ready to die. If they were ready to die to self and sin, if covetousness and the love of pleasure would die, they would not be so bad; they would be led to bring all their powers into exercise for doing the work of the Master, and then it would be a good death. But it is a spiritual death that pervades our churches. There are not those who feel the importance of teaching the members of the church and trying to get workers for the cause of God, to educate them that they may see the importance of putting to the stretch every power and talent that God has given them.

Our sisters can do a good work for the Master. They can work for the sisters in their homes. Our brethren can reach the men. Those who have a little time, in the place of smoking the cigar and enjoying themselves at the saloon, can not only save their money, but their time, and can do a good work for the Master.

I remember that when the converting power of God came upon me in my childhood I wanted everyone else to get the blessing that I had, and I could not rest till I had told them of it. I began to visit with my young companions and went to their houses to talk with them and tell them my experience, how precious the Saviour was to me, and how I wanted to serve Him, and how I wanted them to serve Him also. So I would talk of the preciousness of Christ, and I would say, Won't you kneel down and pray with me? Some would kneel and some would sit in their chairs, but before we gave up, every one would be on their knees and we would pray together for hours, till the last one would say, "I believe that Jesus has forgiven my sins." Sometimes the sun would begin to make its appearance in the heavens before I would give up the struggle.

There is a great power in Jesus. Now when we go into the house we should not begin to talk of frivolous things, but come right to the point and say, I want you to love Jesus for He has first loved you. And as Brother Starr has said, take along the publications and ask them to read. When they see that you are sincere they will not despise any of your efforts. There is a way to reach the hardest hearts. Approach in the simplicity, sincerity, and humility that will help us to reach the souls of those for whom Christ died. We do not want to be negligent in this work.

The plan now under consideration I believe to be one that God will be pleased with. Churches that are now ready to die want someone to devise and plan for them who has the power to set things in operation. But who will do it? There are enough who want to be Christians, and if we will let the leaven begin to work, it will take one and then another, just as the Spirit of God will

## Remarks on Missionary Work

work with us, and we will see that we can reach the people, not by our own smartness, but by the Spirit of God. Yet we want the ability and power that God has given us to be brought into use. We do not want to be novices forever; we want to know how to conduct ourselves properly; we want Christian politeness. And we want to carry it with us in all our work. We do not want any of the sharp corners which may be in our character to be made prominent, but we want to work in humility, so we will forget them, and better characteristics will come in. We want cheerfulness in our work. A great deal depends on the way you meet those whom you go to visit. You can take hold of the hand in such a way as at once to gain the confidence. If you take hold of it with a cold, unimpressive manner, as though you were an iceberg and did not want to be melted, you will find no warmth in return.

When we were on the boat on our way to Europe I met a physician who said, "I want to give you a little advice. You will find a cold, stiff-necked people, and if you will be as stiff you will never do them any good; but if you will go right to them and talk with them no matter how diffident they seem to be, they will meet you all right; talk to them just as you did to me. They will see that you have a heart and will love to talk with you. I love to talk with you about these things; do the same way in England."

You don't want to hold yourselves as though it were a condescension to come in contact with poor families. Talk as though they were as good a piece of humanity as you are. They have little enough light and joy, and why not carry additional joy and light to shine in upon them and fill their hearts? What we want is the tender sympathy of Jesus Christ, and then we can melt our way right into their hearts. We want to clothe ourselves, not with pomposity, but with plain, simple dress, so that they will feel that we are an equal with them, and as though we considered that they were worth saving, and we can melt our way into their hearts.

Now, brethren and sisters, we want the iron taken out of our souls, and we want it taken out of our manner of work. We can educate workers in every church. Don't let the ministers feel that they must do all the talking, and all the laboring; but call on others to lead the meetings occasionally. In doing this they are being educated. Let them take turns in giving Bible readings. This is calling into use the talent which God has given them.

I read of a man who had a corps of workmen over whom he placed an overseer. He had charge of twelve men and they were to dig a trench, and the man came along one day where they were at work, and there was the overseer down in the trench, and the sweat was rolling off from his brow, but the twelve men were looking down into the trench watching him in his labor. The overseer was called up and asked what he was doing down there. "I ordered you to keep twelve men at work. Why have you not done it? Here are your wages."

Now, God has made us teachers of the flock, and He wants us to educate them in every branch of the work, that we may bring in all the talents. Our ministers do the labor instead of educating others to take the responsibility of the cause. The minister's work should be the work of a teacher. One laborer might set twenty to work in less time than it would take him to do the work himself. Let them blunder and make mistakes, and then kindly show them how they can do it better, and then you can be educating, educating, educating, until you have men and women who have experience in the things of God and can carry responsibility, and that is what we have been suffering for. We need men who can bear responsibility, and the best way to gain the experience they need is to engage in this work.

Then if we work for others we will not lack for something to talk about when we assemble together. We will not have to talk about our brethren and think of our self-sufficiency, for we will be working out of those things and getting to be workers for Jesus Christ. If this branch of the work could be taken up in every

## Remarks on Missionary Work

conference and church, I believe we should see in the year to come an elevation, a healthfulness, a different atmosphere in the church. There would not be so many tattlers and gossipers. There would not be so much time for idle tales, and we would see many souls converted to Christ. Why should we not feel an interest for those around us when Christ has given us such an evidence of His love? Why, brethren, God will not leave us. He will let His converting power be upon us. These things will enlarge as the waves from a pebble thrown in the water; the first are small, but they grow larger and larger till they reach the bank.

Brethren, we want to do something to set things in operation for God. We want to do something that will save souls, that at last we may enter into the joy of our Lord, that we may give praises to our Lord that we have been the means of saving some through Him. That some may say, It is through your instrumentality, it is you who saved me through Jesus Christ. That is the way we shall enter into the joy of our Lord. This is the way we want to work. We cannot know here what the effect of our work has been, but we shall see in eternity what we have done for the Master. Shall we plan and devise to carry out these plans to the letter? Then the blessings of the Lord will attend all our labors.

# Morning Talk

*Oct. 24, 1888, MS 9, 1888*

Now our meeting is drawing to a close, and not one confession has been made; there has not been a single break so as to let the Spirit of God in.

Now I was saying what was the use of our assembling here together and for our ministering brethren to come in if they are here only to shut out the Spirit of God from the people? We did hope that there would be a turning to the Lord here. Perhaps you feel that you have all you want.

I have been awake since two o'clock and I have been praying, but I cannot see the work making the advancement that I wish I could. I have been talking and pleading with you, but it does not seem to make any difference with you. As I have told my children, although they are thousands of miles away, when I go to God in prayer for them I know where they are standing in the Christian life, and if they are not living close to God I am alarmed.

Had Brother Kilgore been walking closely with God he never would have walked onto the ground as he did yesterday and made the statement he did in regard to the investigation that is going on. That is, they must not bring in any new light or present any new argument notwithstanding they have been constantly handling the Word of God for years, yet they are not prepared to give a reason of the hope they have because one man is not here. Have we not all been looking into this subject?

I never was more alarmed than at the present time. Now, I have been taken down through the first rebellion, and I saw the workings of Satan and I know something about this matter that God has opened before me, and should not I be alarmed? And then to take the position that because Elder Butler was not here that that subject should not be taken up. I know this is not of God and I shall not feel free until I have told you.

Here was the enemy inculcating his ideas in the hearts of the angels, and they express these ideas that he has inculcated as their own, and Satan takes them and tells them to the other angels as the sentiments of the angels he has been working with, and thus he inculcates his ideas into their minds, and then draws them out of the angels as their own ideas.

Now I am full of pain as I view these things, and how can I help it? Do you think that when I see these things transpiring that I can keep still and say nothing when these things have been shown me? I want to tell you, my brethren, that it is not right to fasten ourselves upon the ideas of any one man.

Now I want to tell you what a good brother said to me as he was about to leave the meeting. He came to me with such a feeling of relief that everything was settled and our old position was all right.

Well, one says, "Your prayers and your TALK run in the channel with Dr. Waggoner." I want to tell you, my brethren, that I have not taken any position; I have had [no] TALK with the doctor nor with anyone on this subject, and am not prepared to take a position yet. By their fruits ye shall know them. I took my brethren and told them just where they were, but they did not believe me, they did not believe they were in any danger.

If Elder Waggoner's views were wrong, what business has anyone to get up and say what they did here yesterday? If we have the truth it will stand. These truths that we have been handling for years—must Elder Butler come and tell us what they are? Now, do let us have common sense. Don't let us leave such an impression on this people. One brother asked me if I thought there was any new light that we should have or any new truths for us? Well, shall we stop searching the Scriptures because we have the light on the law of God and the testimony of His Spirit? No, brethren. I tell you in the fear of God, "Cease ye from man, whose breath is in his nostrils." How can you listen to all that I have been telling you all through these meetings and not know for yourself what is truth? If you will search the Scriptures on your knees, then you will know them and you will be able to give to every man that asketh you a reason of the hope that is within you.

Let us come to God as reasonable beings to know for ourselves what is truth. But if you want to take a position that only one man can explain the truth, I want to tell you that this is not as God would have it. Now, I want harmony. The truth is a unit. But if we fasten to any man we are not taking the position that God would have us [take]. We want to investigate every line of truth, especially if it bears the signet of God. Can you tell in what way God is going to give us new truth?

When I have been made to pass over the history of the Jewish nation and have seen where they stumbled because they did not walk in the light, I have been led to realize where we as a people would be led if we refuse the light God would give us. Eyes have ye but ye see not; ears, but ye hear not. Now, brethren, light has come to us and we want to be where we can grasp it, and God will lead us out one by one to Him. I see your danger and I want to warn you.

Now, this is the last ministers' meeting we will have unless you wish to meet together yourselves. If the ministers will not receive the light, I want to give the people a chance; perhaps they may receive it. God did not raise me up to come across the plains to speak to you and you sit here to question His message and question whether Sister White is the same as she used to be in years gone by. I have in many things gone way back and given you that which was given me in years past, because then you acknowledged that Sister White was right. But somehow it has changed now, and Sister White is different. Just like the Jewish nation.

Now, we did not intimate one word that we did not want that subject taken up. We did want an investigation, but I cannot take my position on either side until I have studied the question. There is the danger God has shown me that there would be a deceitful handling of the Word of God. I have been shown that when debaters handle these truths, unless they have the Spirit of God, they handle them with their own efforts. They will, by making false theories and false statements, build up a structure that will not stand the test of God. This is what the Lord has shown me.

Now, brethren, we want the truth as it is in Jesus. But when anything shall come in to shut down the gate that the waves of truth shall not come in, you will hear my voice wherever it is, if it is in California or in Europe, or wherever I am, because God has given me light and I mean to let it shine. And I have seen that precious souls who would have embraced the truth have been turned away from it because of the manner in which the truth has been handled, because Jesus was not in it. And this is what I have been pleading with you for all the time—we want Jesus. What is the reason the Spirit of God does not come into our meetings? Is it because we have built a barrier around us? I speak decidedly because I want you to realize where you are standing. I want our young men to take a position, not because someone else takes it, but because they understand the truth for themselves.

Here [are] Elder Smith and Elder Van Horn, who have been handling the truth for years, and yet we must not touch this subject because Elder Butler was not here. Elder Kilgore, I was grieved more than I can express to you when I heard you make that remark, because I have lost confidence in you. Now, we want to get right at what God says; all this terrible feeling I don't believe in. Let us go to the Lord for the truth instead of our showing this spirit of combativeness. God has given me light, and you have acknowledged it in times past.

## Morning Talk

Now, the words that were spoken here were that Elder Waggoner was running this meeting. Has he not presented to you the words of the Bible? Why was it that I lost the manuscript and for two years could not find it? God has a purpose in this. He wants us to go to the Bible and get the Scripture evidence. I shall find it again and present it to you. But this investigation must go forward. All the object I had was that the light should be gathered up, and let the Saviour come in.

I don't expect my testimony is pleasing, yet I shall bear it in God's fear. God knows there is a preparation going on here to fit these ministers for the work, and unless we are converted God does not want us. I hope Brother Morrison will be converted and handle the Word of God with meekness and the Spirit of God. These truths will stand just as long as time shall last. You want the eyesalve that you can see, and Jesus will help you if you will come to Him as little children. May God help us to seek Him with all our hearts.

# A Call to a Deeper Study of the Word

*Nov., 1888, MS 15, 1888*

Dear BRETHREN Assembled at GENERAL Conference:

I entreat you to exercise the spirit of Christians. Do not let strong feelings of prejudice arise, for we should be prepared to investigate the Scriptures with unbiased minds, with reverence and candor. It becomes us to pray over matters of difference in views of Scripture. Personal feelings should not be allowed to influence our words or our judgment. It will grieve the Spirit of God if you close your understanding to the light which God sends you.

Dr. Waggoner has spoken to us in a straightforward manner. There is precious light in what he has said. Some things presented in reference to the law in Galatians, if I fully understand his position, do not harmonize with the understanding I have had of this subject; but truth will lose nothing by investigation, therefore I plead for Christ's sake that you come to the living Oracles, and with prayer and humiliation seek God. Everyone should feel that he has the privilege of searching the Scriptures for himself, and he should do this with earnest prayer that God will give him a right understanding of His Word, that he may know from positive evidence that he does know what is truth.

I would have humility of mind, and be willing to be instructed as a child. The Lord has been pleased to give me great light, yet I know that He leads other minds, and opens to them the mysteries of His Word, and I want to receive every ray of light that God shall send me, though it should come through the humblest of His servants.

## 1888 Sermons

Of one thing I am certain, as Christians you have no right to entertain feelings of enmity, unkindness, and prejudice toward Dr. Waggoner, who has presented his views in a plain, straightforward manner, as a Christian should. If he is in error, you should, in a calm, rational, Christlike manner, seek to show him from the Word of God where he is out of harmony with its teachings. If you cannot do this you have no right as Christians to pick flaws, to criticize, to work in the dark, to prejudice minds with your objections. This is Satan's way of working.

Some interpretations of Scripture given by Dr. Waggoner I do not regard as correct. But I believe him to be perfectly honest in his views, and I would respect his feelings and treat him as a Christian gentleman. I have no reason to think that he is not as much esteemed of God as are any of my BRETHREN, and I shall regard him as a Christian brother, so long as there is no evidence that he is unworthy. The fact that he honestly holds some views of Scripture differing from yours or mine is no reason why we should treat him as an offender, or as a dangerous man, and make him the subject of unjust criticism. We should not raise a voice of censure against him or his teachings unless we can present weighty reasons for so doing and show him that he is in error. No one should feel at liberty to give loose rein to the combative spirit.

There are some who desire to have a decision made at once as to what is the correct view on the point under discussion. As this would please Elder B., it is advised that this question be settled at once. But are minds prepared for such a decision? I could not sanction this course, because our BRETHREN are exercised by a spirit which moves their feelings, and stirs their impulses, so as to control their judgment. While under so much excitement as now exists, they are not prepared to make safe decisions.

I know it would be dangerous to denounce Dr. Waggoner's position as wholly erroneous. This would please the enemy. I see the beauty of truth in the

## A Call to a Deeper Study of the Word

presentation of the righteousness of Christ in relation to the law as the doctor has placed it before us. You say, many of you, it is light and truth. Yet you have not presented it in this light heretofore. Is it not possible that through earnest, prayerful searching of the Scriptures he has seen still greater light on some points? That which has been presented harmonizes perfectly with the light which God has been pleased to give me during all the years of my experience. If our ministering BRETHREN would accept the doctrine which has been presented so clearly—the righteousness of Christ in connection with the law—and I know they need to accept this, their prejudices would not have a controlling power, and the people would be fed with their portion of meat in due season. Let us take our Bibles, and with humble prayer and a teachable spirit, come to the great Teacher of the world; let us pray as did David, "Open thou mine eyes, that I may behold wondrous things out of thy law" (Ps. 119:18).

I see no excuse for the wrought-up state of feeling that has been created at this meeting. This is the first time I have had opportunity to listen to anything in reference to this subject. I have had no conversation in regard to it with my son W.C. White, with Dr. Waggoner, or with Elder A.T. Jones. At this meeting I have heard for the first time Dr. Waggoner's reasons for his position. The messages coming from your president at Battle Creek are calculated to stir you up to make hasty decisions and to take decided positions; but I warn you against doing this. You are not now calm; there are many who do not know what they believe. It is perilous to make decisions upon any controverted point without dispassionately considering all sides of the question. Excited feelings will lead to rash movements. It is certain that many have come to this meeting with false impressions and perverted opinions. They have imaginings that have no foundation in truth. Even if the position which we have held upon the two laws is truth, the Spirit of truth will not countenance any such measures to defend it as many of you would take. The spirit that attends the truth should be such as will represent the Author of truth.

Says the apostle James: "Who is a wise man and endued with knowledge among you? Let him shew out of a good conversation his works with meekness of wisdom. But if ye have bitter envying and strife in your hearts, glory not, and lie not against the truth. This wisdom descendeth not from above, but is earthly, sensual, devilish. For where envying and strife is, there is confusion and every evil work. But the wisdom that is from above is first pure, then peaceable, gentle, and easy to be intreated, full of mercy and good fruits, without partiality, and without hypocrisy. And the fruit of righteousness is sown in peace of them that make peace" (James 3:13–18).

The truth must be presented as it is in Jesus; if there are any among us who become stirred up because ideas contrary from what they have believed are presented in this meeting, then stop your unsanctified criticisms and candidly investigate the subject, and it will sanctify the soul.

Two years ago, while in Switzerland, I was addressed in the night season by a voice which said, "Follow me." I thought I arose, and followed my guide. I seemed to be in the Tabernacle at Battle Creek, and my guide gave instructions in regard to many things at the conference. I will give in substance a few things that were said: "The Spirit of God has not had a controlling influence in this meeting. The spirit that controlled the Pharisees is coming in among this people, who have been greatly favored of God."

Many things were spoken which I will not now present to you. I was told that there was need of great spiritual revival among the men who bear responsibilities in the cause of God. There was not perfection in all points on either side of the question under discussion. We must search the Scriptures for evidences of truth. "There are but few, even of those who claim to believe it, that comprehend the third angel's message, and yet

## A Call to a Deeper Study of the Word

this is the message for this time. It is present truth. But how few take up this message in its true bearing, and present it to the people in its power! With many it has but little force."

Said my guide, "There is much light yet to shine forth from the law of God and the gospel of righteousness. This message, understood in its true character, and proclaimed in the Spirit, will lighten the earth with its glory. The great decisive question is to be brought before all nations, tongues, and peoples. The closing work of the third angel's message will be attended with a power that will send the rays of the Sun of Righteousness into all the highways and byways of life, and decisions will be made for God as supreme Governor; His law will be looked upon as the rule of His government."

Many who claim to believe the truth will change their opinions in times of peril, and will take the side of the transgressors of God's law in order to escape persecution. There will be great humbling of hearts before God on the part of every one who remains faithful and true to the end. But Satan will so work upon the unconsecrated elements of the human mind that many will not accept the light in God's appointed way.

I entreat you, BRETHREN, be not like the Pharisees, who were blinded with spiritual pride, self-righteousness, and self-sufficiency, and who because of this were forsaken of God. For years I have been receiving instructions and warnings that this was the danger to our people. Says the Scripture: "Nevertheless among the chief rulers also many believed on him; but because of the Pharisees they did not confess him, lest they should be put out of the synagogue: for they loved the praise of men more than the praise of God" (John 12:42, 43).

There is positive danger that some who profess to believe the truth will be found in a position similar to that of the Jews. They take the ideas of the men they are associated with, not because by searching the Scriptures they conscientiously accept the teachings in doctrine as truth. I entreat you to make God your trust; idolize no man, depend upon no man. Let not your love of man hold them in places of trust that they are not qualified to fill to the glory of God; for man is finite and erring, liable to be controlled by his own opinions and feelings. Self-esteem and self-righteousness are coming in upon us, and many will fall because of unbelief and unrighteousness, for the grace of Christ is not ruling in the hearts of many.

We are to be ever searching for the truth as for hidden treasures. I entreat you, close not the door of the heart for fear some ray of light shall come to you. You need greater light, you need a clearer understanding of the truth which you carry to the people. If you do not see light yourselves, you will close the door; if you can you will prevent the rays of light from coming to the people. Let it not be said of this highly favored people, "Ye entered not in yourselves, and them that were entering in ye hindered" (Luke 11:52). All these lessons are given for the benefit of those upon whom the ends of the world are come.

I have been shown that Jesus will reveal to us precious old truths in a new light, if we are ready to receive them; but they must be received in the very way in which the Lord shall choose to send them. With humble, softened hearts, with respect and love for one another, search your Bibles. The light may not come in accordance with plans that men may devise. But all who reverence the Word of God just as it reads, all who do His will to the best of their ability, will know of the doctrine, whether it be of God, notwithstanding the efforts of the enemy to confuse minds and to make uncertain the Word of God. God calls every man's attention to His living Oracles. Let no one quench the Spirit of God by wresting the Scriptures, by putting human interpretations upon His inspired Word; and let no one pursue an unfair course, keep in the dark, not willing to open their ears to hear and yet free to comment and quibble and sow their doubts of that which they will not candidly take time to hear.

## A Call to a Deeper Study of the Word

Let men be careful how they handle the Word of inspiration, which has been preserved for ages through the power of God. If men were themselves controlled by the Holy Spirit they would bring heart and soul to the task, searching and digging in the mines of God for precious ore. They would be eager to come into harmony with the writings of inspired men. If they are not controlled by the Spirit of God, they will give evidence of this by caviling over His word and by sitting in judgment upon its teachings just as did the Jews.

We should guard against the influence of men who have trained themselves as debaters, for they are in continual danger of handling the Word of God deceitfully. There are men in our churches all through the land who will pervert the meaning of the Scripture to make a sharp point and overcome an opponent. They do not reverence the Sacred Word. They put their own construction upon its utterances. Christ is not formed within, the hope of glory. They are educated critics, but spiritual truths can only be spiritually discerned. These men are ever ready and equipped to oppose at a moment's notice anything that is contrary to their own opinions. They handle the Scriptures in an unwise way, and bring self into everything they do.

"And the servant of the Lord must not strive; but be gentle unto all men, apt to teach, patient, in meekness instructing those that oppose themselves; if God peradventure will give them repentance to the acknowledging of the truth; and that they may recover themselves out of the snare of the devil, who are taken captive by him at his will" (2 Tim. 2:24–26). The servant of the Lord must not strive, but must teach the Word of God in the manner that God has ordained. Any other way is not God's way, and will create confusion.

Brother Morrison is a debater; he is a man who has not had a daily, living experience in the meekness and lowliness of Christ. He is in danger of making false issues, and of treating them as realities. He will create strife, and the result will be dissensions and bickerings. He has many things to overcome, and if he fails to overcome them, he will make shipwreck of faith, as did Elder Canright. It is dangerous to cherish feelings of self-sufficiency. He must have the meekness of Christ; the sanctifying power of the truth must be brought into the sanctuary of his soul: then he will be a polished instrument in the hands of God to do His work.

It is a matter of deep concern to us whether or not we are perfecting a Christian character, growing in grace and in the knowledge of our Lord Jesus Christ. If we are daily learners in the school of Christ we shall be daily obtaining an experience in Christian life, and we shall not be self-sufficient and self-exalted. We shall be as humble as little children, and there will be a nourishing power in our words which will drop as the dew. The fruits of righteousness, sown in peace of them that make peace, will then appear.

Growth in grace will give Brother Morrison increased ability to comprehend the deep mysteries of the gospel. Those who are in so great a degree unacquainted with Christ are ignorant of the spirit they cherish. They will be dry and Christless. The knowledge of Christ and His word is the foundation and fullness of all knowledge. Many workers are not now fitted for the position of trust they occupy. They must be transformed by the grace of Christ. God wants to give our BRETHREN another spirit. Without this change they will carry the spirit of irreverence for God and His living Oracles into their work; and if this mold is put upon the work, it will dishonor God. The subduing, softening influence of the grace of Christ must fashion and mold character; then it will be a pleasure to deal justly, to love mercy, and to walk humbly with God.

The debating spirit has come into the ranks of Sabbathkeepers to take the place of the Spirit of God. They have placed finite men where God should be, but nothing can suffice for us but to have Christ dwell in our hearts by faith. The truth must become ours. Christ must be our Saviour by an experimental knowledge. We should know by faith what it is to have our

## A Call to a Deeper Study of the Word

sins pardoned, and to be born again. We must have a higher, deeper wisdom than man's to guide us amid the perils surrounding our pathway. The Spirit of Christ must be in us just as the blood is in the body, circulating through it as a vitalizing power.

Our greatest fear should be that we may be found rebelling against God's Word, which is to be our guide amid all the perils of the last days. We must be sure that we are on the Lord's side, that we have the truth as it is in Jesus. With the grace of God in the soul, we may be secure anywhere, strong in the Lord, and in the power of His might.

We would discourage the discipline that tends to make persons debaters. We urge you not to connect young men who are learning to be teachers of Bible truth with one who has a debating spirit, for they will surely receive the wrong mold of character. The habitual debater is so accustomed to beclouding and turning aside evidence, and even the Scriptures, from the true meaning to win his point, that everything that does not strike him favorably and is not in harmony with his ideas he will combat, caviling at God's inspired Word.

There is too little dependence upon God. When God would have a special work done for the advancement of the truth, He will impress men to work in the mines of truth with prayerful earnestness to discover the precious ore. These men will have Christlike perseverance. They will not fail or be discouraged. They will sink self out of sight in Jesus. Men will go forth in the spirit and power of Elijah to prepare the way for the second advent of the Lord Jesus Christ. It is their work to make crooked things straight. Some things must be torn down, some things must be built up. The old treasures must be reset in a framework of truth. They are to preach God's Word; their testimony must not be molded by the opinions and ideas that have been regarded as sound, but by the Word of God, which liveth and abideth forever. They are to lift up Christ and call sinners to repentance. They are to practice the graces of Christ, to pursue a straightforward course, breaking down skepticism and urging upon all their personal responsibility to be kind and courteous, to do good and to win souls to Jesus.

The Scripture should not be treated in a debating style. Those who have educated themselves as debaters have so increased their spirit of combativeness that they are ready to cavil over the Word of God, to resist and oppose everything that disagrees with their ideas or opinions. They are in their element when an opportunity is offered for them to question and criticize, for it is natural for them to be ready for battle at any time. They will play upon words, misinterpret and misstate, because this has become a settled habit with them, a second nature. Nothing is safe in their hands. Now, the Lord desires that those who are in this condition should be converted, that they become as little children—simple, meek, teachable, and Christlike.

We must have the power of God to soften and change the rugged traits of our character, that we may be susceptible to the influence of truth. We should look upon the Word of God with reverence, as something sacred. Christ is true, and without Him we know nothing as we ought to know it. We are lacking in the spirituality of true religion.

When the Jews took the first step in the rejection of Christ, they took a dangerous step. When afterward evidence accumulated that Jesus of Nazareth was the Messiah, they were too proud to acknowledge that they had erred. So with the people of our day who reject the truth. They do not take time to investigate candidly, with earnest prayer, the evidences of the truth, and they oppose that which they do not understand. Just like the Jews, they take it for granted they have all the truth, and feel a sort of contempt for anyone who should suppose they had more correct ideas than themselves of what is truth. All the evidence produced they decide shall not weigh a straw with them, and they tell others that the doctrine is not true, and afterward, when they see as light evidence they were so forward to

## A Call to a Deeper Study of the Word

condemn, they have too much pride to say "I was wrong;" they still cherish doubt and unbelief, and are too proud to acknowledge their convictions. Because of this, they take steps that lead to results of which they have never dreamed.

Those who have not been in the habit of thinking and investigating for themselves, believe certain doctrines because their associates with them in the work believe them. They resist the truth without going to the Scriptures for themselves to learn what is truth. Because those in whom they have had confidence oppose the light, they oppose it, not knowing they are rejecting the counsel of God against themselves.

God has a work to do in our world that many finite minds do not see or understand, and when God unfolds truth to His people, and it does not come in harmony with their ideas, many are ready to despise and reject it. I entreat you, BRETHREN, reverence your Bible. Plead with God for light. Fast and pray in your closet upon your knees. Ask God to lead you into all truth. Tell Him that you want the truth as it is in Jesus. It is not wise for one of these young men to commit himself to a decision at this meeting, where opposition, rather than investigation, is the order of the day. The Scriptures must be your study, then you will know that you have the truth. Open your heart that God might write the truth upon its tablets.

One who would be a teacher of sacred things should not go forth to work with the people without a full assurance that he has the truth. He should not go forth feeling that perhaps the doctrines which he advocates may not all be substantiated by the Bible. Anything short of a full conviction that what he presents is truth will make his preaching powerless, unless he has the presumption to put forth mere assertions as conclusive evidence. This is unfair, and yet this has often been done by sharp debaters. You should give your authority to the people from God's Word. You should not believe any doctrine simply because another says it is truth. You should not believe it because Elder Smith, or Elder Kilgore, or Elder Van Horn, or Elder Haskell says it is truth, but because God's voice has declared it in His living Oracles.

Truth will triumph gloriously, and those who have received the truth because God has revealed it in His Word will triumph with it. Those who neglect to search for evidence for themselves, and rely upon what someone else says, will not have root in themselves, and will not be able to give a reason of the hope that is within them. God's commands must be heard. He says, "Go forward." There are large fields to be explored. There are mines to be discovered in which are precious jewels of truth. Let no one close these mines, and cease to dig for the truth lest they should have to cast aside some preconceived idea or opinion. No, BRETHREN, we want to know the truth; and God forbid that any of you should turn from precious truths simply because you do not want to believe them.

No one must be permitted to close the avenues whereby the light of truth shall come to the people. As soon as this shall be attempted, God's Spirit will be quenched, for that Spirit is constantly at work to give fresh and increased light to His people through His Word. Let the love of Christ reign in hearts here. Let all yield themselves to that heavenly power which alone can create unity by quelling selfish ambitions and human pride. When the Spirit of God comes in, love will take the place of variance, because Jesus is love; if His spirit were cherished here our meeting would be like a stream in the desert.

Has the truth as it is in Jesus been received into the heart? Have the mind of God and His ways become our mind and our ways? Is the law of God our standard? If it is, its principles will be wrought out in our life. Wherever the love of Jesus reigns there is peace with God, joy in God; and the love and joy are reflected to others. We cannot afford to be deceived by a semblance, a form. The truth of the Bible may be read, and we may think that a form of words will accomplish that which only the Spirit of God can accomplish by its

## A Call to a Deeper Study of the Word

converting, transforming power. We may hold certain points of truth firmly and yet refuse to let in any fresh rays of light which God may send to show us the beauty of the truth. It is dangerous for us to take a step in uncertainty. We should not reject or oppose the views of our fellow laborers because they do not agree with our ideas until we have used every means in our power to find out whether or not they are truth, comparing scripture with scripture.

If we do otherwise, a combative spirit will arise at the first approach of anything that differs from our views. We may be led on by the enemy to take a position against the truth, because it does not come in a way to suit us; and in the spirit of the deceived Jews, we shall resist the light which God sends; and that light, instead of being the blessing which heaven meant it to be to us, to advance us in spirituality and in the knowledge of God, will become a stumbling-block, over which we shall be constantly falling. We shall become irritated and indignant, for enmity is in our heart against God's truth. If evidence is afterwards presented from the Scriptures, it will not be received by him who has rejected light. The men of Nazareth opened their hearts to unbelief, and as the result they rejected Christ. The combative spirit will rise against the truth, and unfair means will be taken to influence others, and to make it of none effect. The Lord would have our intellect sanctified, elevated, ennobled, that we may distinguish truth from error, and bring the truth into the soul temple, that it may exercise an influence upon our spirit and character.

The most terrible thing that could come to us as people is the fatal deception that was the ruin of Chorazin and Bethsaida. They had great light, great privileges and blessings. Jesus was with them, but they did not appreciate or receive the light He gave them. They were not made better by it.

I would warn all my ministering BRETHREN, and especially the young, never to touch an infidel book, never to present infidel cavils. Some have thought it essential to understand these, that they might know how to meet objectors. In our college, debaters have been educated by considering objections to the Bible. This has sometimes been done by our students for the purpose of bringing the light of truth in contrast with infidel arguments. In times when the soul is under temptation, Satan causes the seeds of doubt that are thus sown to germinate, and they blossom into fruit. Discipline of this order is a dangerous discipline for our students. Never give the least sanction to the presentation of infidel arguments. Turn from them as you would from a serpent, for there is concealed in them a sting that would wound the soul.

Principles and practices must be strictly guarded. Habits are formed by training the mind in a certain of action. What we do once, we do more readily the second time, and we learn to pursue a certain course by force of habit. If we are trained to cavil, we shall be trained to doubt and uncertainty. When Jesus is not abiding in the soul, the natural tendency to doubt, question, and criticize will extend to God's Word, as well as to the testimonies, and the habit of caviling will ruin the soul. In place of godly fear and holy reverence in handling the Scriptures, there will be a forward, bold assumption, a proud, boasting spirit that loves to strive, and the most sacred things will be lightly regarded, the most sacred feelings will be trampled upon. God has but little to do with such workers.

We are to hold fast every jot and tittle of the truth revealed to us in the living oracles; but we are not to think that we now have a knowledge of all the truth that there is for us. We may well ask whither we are drifting. Even the inspiration of the Scriptures has been under the judgment of finite man, and they have dealt with the oracles of God in the same manner as they have with the testimonies of the Spirit of God, cutting and carving them at will, as it pleased them, and in so doing, making them of none effect. Those who do this, know not what they are doing.

## A Call to a Deeper Study of the Word

Unless there is most earnest seeking of the Lord, unless there is zealous work of repentance, darkness will come upon minds, and the darkness will be in proportion to the light which has not been appreciated. Unless there is less of self, and far more of the Holy Spirit to take control of the minds and hearts of men who have stood in the foremost rank, there will be a failure on their part to walk out in harmony with the opening providences of God; they will question and quibble over any light that the Lord may send, and will turn away from the teachings of Christ, confiding in themselves, and trusting in their supposed knowledge of what is truth. As the Jews refused the light of the world, so many of those who claim to believe the present truth will refuse light which the Lord will send to His people.

[Revelation 3:14-21 quoted.] Shall its solemn warnings have no weight with us?

Never let Satan have the control of your powers. As a people we need humility. In this conference we are sowing seeds that will yield a harvest, and the results will be as enduring as eternity. Young workers are watching to see what spirit you manifest in this meeting, and how you treat those who hold views that differ from yours. You know that precious light has shone forth in connection with the law of God, as the righteousness of Christ has been presented with that law. Dr. Waggoner has opened to you precious light, not new, but old light which has been lost sight of by many minds, and is now shining forth in clear rays. Let a spirit of fairness come in. Though you think his ideas upon this subject may not be all sound, do not make false statements, do not mistake his words; place him in no false light; maintain the spirit of Christ; keep the commandments of God, love God supremely, and your neighbor as yourself.

God's law reads, "Thou shalt not bear false witness." I hope none will go from this meeting repeating the false statements that have been circulated here, or carrying with them the spirit which has been here manifested. It has not been of Christ; it has come from another source. All who have the truth can afford to be fair. See to it, my BRETHREN, that words coming from finite man are not received as the voice of God. We want to be Christians. We should pray and study our Bibles more. Nothing is safe that does not bear the credentials of heaven. Let God be true, and every man a liar. His word is infinite, and every man will find that it is sure and steadfast forever.

We invite you to view the complete
selection of titles we publish at:

www.LNFBooks.com

or write or email us your praises,
reactions, or thoughts about this
or any other book we publish at:

**TEACH Services, Inc.**

P.O. Box 954

Ringgold, GA 30736

info@TEACHServices.com